Che Guevara

Pocket BIOGRAPHIES

Series Editor C.S. Nicholls

Highly readable brief lives of those who have played a significant part in history, and whose contributions still influence contemporary culture.

Pocket BIOGRAPHIES

Che Guevara

ANDREW SINCLAIR

SUTTON PUBLISHING

First published in the United Kingdom in 1998 by
Sutton Publishing Limited · Phoenix Mill
Thrupp · Stroud · Gloucestershire · GL5 2BU

Reprinted in 2001, 2002, 2003

British Library Cataloguing in Publication Data
A catalogue record for this book is available from the British Library

ISBN 0 7509 1847 0

Typeset in 13/17pt Perpetua.
Typesetting and origination by
Sutton Publishing Limited.
Printed in Great Britain by
J.H. Haynes & Co. Ltd, Sparkford.

CONTENTS

CHRONOLOGY

1928   **14 June.** Ernesto ('Che') Guevara de la Serna is
              born in Rosario, Argentina, the first of
              five children.

1932   Because of Che's asthma, the Guevara family
              moves to Alta Gracia.

1948   Studies medicine in Buenos Aires.

1951–2   Travels with Alberto Granado by motorcycle
              around South and Central America.

1953   Qualifies as a doctor and leaves Argentina.
              Observes the effects of the Bolivian Revolution.

1954   Analyses the American-backed coup against the
              radical government of Jacobo Arbenz in
              Guatemala. Escaping to Mexico, he enlists and
              trains with the Cuban revolutionaries led by Fidel
              Castro. Marries a Peruvian revolutionary, Hilda
              Gadea, and has a daughter, Hildita.

1956   Lands with 82 Cuban exiles on the yacht
              Granma and begins from the Sierra Maestra a
              guerrilla war against the dictator
              Fulgencio Batista.

1958   Meets his second wife, Aleida March de la Torre.

1959   With the flight of Batista and the fall of Havana,
              Fidel Castro sets up a revolutionary government

in Cuba. Che is made the Governor of the
National Bank and tries to apply socialist
economic planning to Cuban conditions.

1961   Minister for Industry. Castro's regime withstands
the American-backed invasion by Cuban exiles at
the Bay of Pigs. Che becomes a roving ambassador
for Castro round the Communist and socialist
powers, and across the non-aligned and Third
World countries during the Cold War between
the United States and Russia.

1962   After the Cuban Missile Crisis, Che turns against
Russia, the chief supporter of the Cuban
economy, in favour of the rural revolution of Mao
Zedong in China.

1965   Leaves Cuba to lead the international revolution
against imperialism. Travels through Africa and is
defeated in the Congo by western mercenaries.

1966   Returns to the Caribbean and Latin America to
encourage armed revolutions there. Increasingly
estranged from Cuban and Russian policy, he
leaves to begin a guerrilla war in Bolivia.

1967   After training and fighting for nine months, the
failing Guevara is captured on 8 October 1967
and executed the following day.

1968   Across the world, student and urban revolutions
break out, inspired by the example of Che
Guevara. They are all suppressed by
government forces.

BACKGROUND OF A REVOLUTIONARY

'I was born in Argentina, I fought in Cuba, and I began to be a revolutionary in Guatemala.'[1] These words summed up what Che Guevara called his autobiographical synthesis. They also described a continent always in tension between reactionary governments and utopian rebels. Guevara was the first man since Simon Bolívar with a serious plan to unite the squabbling neighbours of Latin America. His own life displayed all the contradictions of his place and time.

He was the child of aristocrats, the first son of Ernesto Guevara Lynch and Celia de la Serna y Llosa, one of whose family had been a Spanish Viceroy of Peru, another a celebrated Argentinian general. The Spanish and Irish Guevaras and Lynchs had come as immigrants to Argentina twelve generations before, while the de la Sernas had much property and radical sympathies. Che Guevara's grandmother, Ana Lynch, also had American blood and was born in California, and his mother Celia, with her reforming beliefs, was the dominant influence on Che's life until he met Fidel Castro.

Ernesto Guevara de la Serna was born prematurely on 14 June 1928 in his father's birthplace at Rosario: he was later nicknamed Che. Subject to pneumonia and asthma, he was taken to the mountains at Alta Gracia on the foothills of the Córdoba Sierra to help his breathing. His mother Celia taught the wheezing boy to read and write, while his father pursued his business in construction engineering and shipbuilding. Che went briefly to state schools. His radical mother helped him to get on with whoever was there, but the huge difference between the privileged children like himself and the rest of his schoolmates from poor backgrounds was made clear. His uncle, the poet Cayetano Córdova Itúrburu, a member of the Communist Party, reported on the Spanish Civil War, sending back to Argentina his dispatches from the Republican Front. These influenced the young Che, who never revolted against his free-thinking home, but against the oppression of his continent. As Ricardo Rojo, a friend of the family, testified, certain things were taken for granted in the Guevara household – 'a passion for justice, the rejection of Fascism, religious indifference, an interest in literature and love of poetry, and a prejudice against money and the ways of making it.'[2] This home conditioning naturally led to a sense of rebelliousness, which, once he could understand the social problems of South America, was to make Che into a revolutionary.

Che acted as if he were a youth as a boy and a man as a youth. A classmate found him 'incredibly sure of himself and totally independent in his opinions . . . very dynamic, restless and unconventional.'[3] To a teacher, Che 'looked and acted much older than he was, and was clearly already grown up with a definite personality, moody and undisciplined, but extremely mature.'[4] While he was still at secondary school, his friends were university students who accepted him as their equal. His realism already outweighed their wish for romantic protest. On one occasion, when asked to take to the streets in a political demonstration, he refused coldly, 'Go out into the streets so that the police can hit us with their clubs? Nothing doing. I'll go and demonstrate only if you give me a gun.'[5] Such an assessment of the situation in his youth made Che's later assertion plausible, that a man at fifteen already knows what he wants to die for and is not afraid of giving his life if he has found an ideal which makes the sacrifice easy.

However, Che had not yet found an ideal. With General Franco's victory in Spain, Fascist movements emerged in many South American nations. Against the reactionaries stood the Guevara family, who founded a local branch of Acción Argentina and enrolled Che as a youth member. With the outbreak of the Second World War, these radical groups opposed the local backers of Hitler. Acción Argentina also opposed the rise to power of Colonel Juan Domingo Perón after the end of the global conflict, although Che was then more interested in sport than politics. He learned to play football and rugby, as a scrum-half, although his asthma often forced him to leave the field. By temperament, he looked on difficulties as tests of will. Disabilities were to be defeated, barriers to be broken. He reduced a six-year university course to three years, passing sixteen major examinations in six months in spite of forty-five serious asthma attacks. His aunt said of this time, 'We would listen to him gasping, studying as he lay on the floor to ease his breathing, but he never complained. For him, it was a challenge.'[6] By the greatest irony of all, a board of army doctors declared him unfit for any sort of military service, once he was eighteen. His training in warfare had to wait a while. 'There is justice after all,' his mother later said.

In 1946 Che decided to study medicine in Buenos Aires, although Perón was now installed as the President of the Republic of Argentina. His grandmother, Ana Lynch, had died of a stroke and his beloved mother Celia had breast cancer, so he may have been trying to compensate for their sufferings and his own fight against asthmatic attacks. He wanted to find remedies for human ills. He could not see pain or death without wanting to strike at the root cause of it all. He had no resignation in him. He could not stand passive acceptance of suffering. His nature was to challenge, even the impossible.

Yet at the Faculty of Medicine in Buenos Aires, Che was more of a humanitarian than a revolutionary. He did not join the student groups opposed to Perón. He later declared that he had no social preoccupations in his adolescence and failed to support the political and student struggle in Argentina. He left his commitments open; travel and observation would later determine his choices. His motorcycle would be his Rosinante towards a quixotic liberty, that would later become revolutionary. When Che's *Motorcycle Diaries* were published posthumously, his father affirmed in a prologue what later became evident, that his son was to follow the path of the *conquistadores* Cortés, Alvarado and Pizarro, but with quite a different purpose.

With his close friend Alberto Granado, Che set off on his quest for a continental solution on a 500 cc Norton, nicknamed *La Poderosa II.* 'Why don't we go to North America?' was the question. The answer lay on the seats of the motorcycle. The pair set off for a hobo's tour of the whole continent, labouring as truck-drivers, porters, doctors and dishwashers. At one time Che was even a guard for a North American mining company in Chile. But the most telling job for the two Argentines was in a leper colony at San Pablo on the Amazon. There Che saw that the highest kinds of human solidarity and loyalty were formed among lonely and desperate men. Che ended the trip starving in Miami, before returning to Buenos Aires to complete his medical degree.

This grand tour at subsistence level was the evidence and basis for Che's feeling that he knew the Americans and their problems. He stated later that he had never felt like a foreigner anywhere. 'I felt Guatemalan in Guatemala, Mexican in Mexico, Peruvian in Peru.' The journey also began to change him into a radical. In a speech in 1960 he remembered the beginnings of his metamorphosis.

Because of the conditions in which I travelled, I came into close contact with poverty and hunger and disease. I discovered that I was unable to cure sick children through lack of means, and I saw the degradation of under-nourishment and constant repression. In this way, I began to realise that there was another thing which was as important as being a famous researcher or making a great contribution to medical science and that was to help those people.[7]

The rough conditions of travel had another effect. They proved to Che that he could endure great hardship and privation – the existence on the margins of survival necessary to any guerrilla fighter. His friends noticed that he could live in the most sinister places and still keep his sense of humour. He only tolerated a travelling companion who could walk huge distances, forget about clothing and go without money. He could also manage to keep moving, even when he had not eaten for three days. Being poor among the poor made Che feel their indignation against their exploiters, their comradeship among themselves, and led him to the self-discipline which he needed to become one of their leaders.

Two months after qualifying as a doctor in 1953 with a thesis on allergies, he threw away his career – to his father's annoyance. He left Argentina never to return, escaping his home and Perón's dictatorship in search of his destiny. With another friend, Carlos Ferrer, he went to Bolivia, which was being ruled by the first effective reform government in its history. The new régime nationalized the country's tin mines, perhaps the largest and worst-run in the world, and distributed the wasteland of the barren *altiplano* among the Indians, who had held no claim to their own soil since the Spanish conquest in the sixteenth century. Che was not yet a Marxist nor a revolutionary; according to his friend Ricardo Rojo, who was also in La Paz, Che's chief interests were still medicine and archaeology, not politics. Yet this first-hand contact with a large programme of social change in action turned Che towards the ideas of revolutionary progress. Paradoxically enough, Bolivia was the country which both inspired Che's political career and would kill him.

When Che visited the tin mines, a leader of the Bolivian Communist Party, Mario Monje, described him as 'a kind of orchid seed, looking for a place to settle'.[8] Che knew, however, that the Bolivian revolution was doomed to partial failure. He and Rojo interviewed the Minister for Peasant Affairs and were disappointed by him. Standing in the street in front of a statue of Bolívar, Che said:

The question is one of fighting the causes and not just being satisfied with getting rid of the effects. This revolution is bound to fail if it doesn't manage to break down the spiritual isolation of the Indians, if it doesn't succeed in reaching deep inside them, stirring them right down to the bone, and giving them back their stature as human beings. Otherwise, what's the use?[9]

The two friends also visited the great mines of Oruro and Catavi. The Minister of Mines, Juan Lechín, had claimed that the revolution was more deep-rooted in Bolivia than even in China, but Che remained unconvinced. The fact that the government had raised the wages of the miners when it had nationalized the mines made Che gloomy. He thought that it was a grave error to confuse the necessities of a nation in arms with the bribes paid to workers when a business changed hands. For a pittance the miners had lessened the material and moral reserves of a revolution that would need every reserve it had in the end. None of Che's friends in Bolivia could change his mind.

Che and Rojo left Bolivia by truck with a party of Indians, heading for Peru. Rojo's account of the Indians' reactions to himself and Che was a prophecy of the reactions that Che would meet as a guerrilla in Bolivia fifteen years later.

The trip was an indispensable one in our education about
the America of the Indians. We entered a hostile world, we
were trapped between bundles and people who looked like
bundles. There was silence. Jolts, bruises and silence. We
found out that it was impossible to try and show our
sympathy before those eyes of metal which stared at us,
those lips as tight and forbidding as a vice that refused to
reply to our questions. . . . We couldn't communicate
in any human way with the Indians, yet the guards at
the Peruvian border were absolutely convinced that we had
turned their heads with ideas about agrarian revolution.[10]

With other Argentine students, Che and Rojo
travelled on to tropical Guayaquil, where Che was
laid low by ill health and poverty. There he made a
decision that he never revoked. He had sworn to
join his friend Granado at the leper colony at San
Pablo, but he needed little persuasion by the
Argentine students to continue on with them to
Guatemala, where there was another revolution in
action. As Rojo said, Che was not yet a Marxist and
was not yet really interested in politics, but another
friend noticed that Che already seemed to feel
responsible for the world's injustices. He was
groping his way towards the root cause of all the
misery he had seen and sometimes shared among
the poor of Latin America. Yet he was still unread in

political philosophy. He saw the evidence of exploitation, but not the method of changing the system.

Juan Bosch, who later became a short-term and reforming President of the Dominican Republic, also met Che on his travels. He found that Che was intensely preoccupied with what he saw. He seemed dissatisfied with all solutions proposed up to that time, and when he was asked specific questions, he criticized all parties, but he never defined his own position. Yet Bosch was convinced by the way that Che answered questions that he had not yet become a Communist. His heart was moving before his mind. His sense of liberty was still in conflict with his feeling that a bureaucracy might have to run a socialist state. He needed to see another revolution in action and to study revolutionary thought, in order to find a system for change.

Jacobo Arbenz Guzmán, who led the new revolutionary government in Guatemala, had a lasting influence on Che. Backed by a coalition of young army officers and intellectuals, Arbenz had decided to tackle the most dangerous reform of all. When Che arrived in 1953, Arbenz was redistributing to the Indians and the peasants large areas of the land just nationalized from the United Fruit Company. The danger of the reform lay in provoking a counter-attack by large interests in the United States, for the United Fruit Company had long been used to controlling what it called 'banana republics' for the benefit of its American shareholders. Arbenz brought Che up against the realities of North American economic power. He also defined the political character of his régime in terms that were not materialist. 'Man is not just a stomach,' Arbenz declared. 'We believe that, above all, he hungers for dignity.' This attitude was central to Che's later thinking, which elaborated this same concept that the socialist is not and cannot be a materialist in outlook, because true socialism is a negation of materialism, even though Marx himself had declared for dialectical materialism. Throughout his life Che remained an admirer of Arbenz and his programme.

Yet Che's admiration was not enough. His wish to work for the revolution as a doctor in the jungles of the Petén fell foul of his distrust of bureaucracy. He visited the minister in charge of the Public Health Department and seemed to be accepted until he was asked for his card. 'What card?' Guevara asked. The minister replied that naturally Che had to be a member of the Guatemalan Labour Party, another name for the local Communist Party. Che replied that he was a revolutionary and did not believe that affiliations of that sort meant anything. Anyway, he would never join the Party from a sense of obligation, only from a sense of conviction. He did not get the job and had to survive by selling encyclopedias and working in a laboratory. He was also helped by a relationship with a Peruvian revolutionary, Hilda Gadea, of Indian and Chinese as well as Spanish ancestry. She supported Che and had a heart of platinum, as he wrote to his mother. They later wed in Mexico and had one daughter, Hildita, but their marriage would always be the victim of their cause.

The downfall of the Arbenz régime in 1954 was Che's baptism in the practical techniques of revolution and counter-revolution. In retaliation for the seizure of the plantations of the United Fruit Company, the Eisenhower government had permitted the Central Intelligence Agency to begin organizing and financing a *coup d'état* in Guatemala. Three factors were working in favour of the CIA plot. First, the Guatemalan army officers behind Arbenz were becoming discouraged by the slow pace of the revolution, which had not yet had the time to win the support and confidence of the Indian masses. Secondly, the régime itself was split by personal ambitions which hid themselves in ideological differences. Thirdly, the middle classes were becoming frightened by the government's open defiance of the United States.

By the end of January Arbenz was accusing the Eisenhower administration of organizing an invasion of Guatemala by exiles. This accusation, however, did not unite the country behind Arbenz. It merely accentuated the divisions in his own party and the fears of the Guatemalans. In June Guatemala was invaded by the troops of Castillo Armas, trained by the CIA and well equipped. The Guatemalan army refused to arm the people, for fear of losing its own position of power. The Arbenz régime fell apart in bickering and recriminations. 'We are like the Spanish Republic,' Guevara concluded, 'betrayed from within and without, but we did not fall with the same dignity.'[11]

This collapse brought out the activist in Che. For the first time, he joined the resistance. He had a strategy and plan of defence, but he could not find any group to adopt it. He encouraged the Guatemalans as much as he could, urged them to fight for their revolution and transported weapons from place to place. But nothing he did was of any use. As the Argentine ambassador told him, he could not do by himself what the government was not willing to do.

When Arbenz weakly resigned and Armas took over, Che had to flee for asylum to the Argentine embassy, as he had already been marked for execution. There he stayed as a virtual prisoner for almost two months, analysing the failure of the revolution.

The French radical intellectual, Régis Debray, who would be imprisoned in Bolivia for trying to join Guevara on his last expedition to that country, declared that 'for a revolutionary, failure is a springboard. As a source of theory it is richer than victory: it accumulates experience and knowledge.'[12] Che's attempts at action in Guatemala may have proved futile, but he had tried to act. He described himself at the time as being defeated, yet united in his pain with all the Guatemalans, and 'seeking a way to recreate a future for that bleeding land'. As with Antaeus, Che's downfall led him to rise again even more strong; a defeat merely meant more preparation for the victory next time. Above all, it meant more faith in the people, whom Arbenz had not trusted enough to arm or integrate into the political structure of the country.

If the CIA had won a temporary victory for North American financial interests in Guatemala, it had also conjured up a deadly enemy. The naked overthrow of a socialist country by a capitalist plot pushed Che into the study of Marx and Lenin. All the personal hatred that Che felt for the enemies of Arbenz, the subverters of his government and his land reform, seemed to be demonstrated in the explanation of the past and present history of the world found in the Marxist version of imperialism. A poor and exploited country with a government that was trying to improve the lot of the masses had been deliberately attacked by a rich capitalist power that depended for its dividends on the exploitation of that poor country. This was a textbook example of the worst form of imperialism in practice. For Che Guevara, the United States became the villain of his personal experience and his new ideology. As Che's first wife Hilda Gadea would write, 'It was Guatemala which finally convinced him of the necessity for armed struggle and for taking the initiative against imperialism. By the time he left, he was sure of this.'[13]

Che left for Mexico to study theories of revolution. In Mexico City, where he lived on the margins of existence, he read the complete works of Marx and Lenin 'and a whole pantheon of Marxist thinkers'. He particularly studied books dealing with military strategy in the Spanish Civil War. Many of the refugees from that war had been given asylum in

Mexico City, so open in welcoming the losers of foreign battles and so niggardly in feeding them. Under the pressure of hunger and study and experience, Che became a committed radical. He even tested his asthma in preparation for combat by climbing Mount Popocatépetl. The slow progress of social reform in Mexico, still limping forward after many decades of revolutionary rule, did not impress him. 'The Mexican revolution is dead,' he declared. 'It has been dead a long time and we hadn't even noticed.'

This new and fierce radicalism made Che ready in the summer of 1955 for his meeting with Fidel Castro. Castro had been jailed and exiled from Cuba for leading a failed coup against the dictator, Fulgencio Batista. Castro was looking for a dedicated group of revolutionaries for a second attempt to overthrow Batista. On the night of his first meeting with Fidel, Che joined the Cuban expedition. He was the second to join after Fidel's brother, Raúl. 'It would have taken very little to persuade me', Che wrote later, 'to join any revolution against a tyranny.' The price would be his first marriage. 'I lost my husband', Hilda Gadea later said, 'to the Cuban revolution.'

When Fidel Castro came to pay his tribute to

Che Guevara, he recorded the first meeting between them in terms which owed much to hindsight. In 1955 both men were still romantic and amateur revolutionaries, not revolutionary rulers and experts. But later, Fidel wrote of Che:

> He was filled with a profound spirit of hatred and loathing for imperialism, not only because his political awareness was already considerably developed, but also because shortly before, he had had the opportunity of witnessing the criminal imperialist intervention in Guatemala through the mercenaries who aborted the revolution in that country. A man like Che did not require elaborate arguments. It was enough for him to know that there were men determined to struggle against that situation, arms in hand; it was enough for him to know that those men were inspired by genuinely revolutionary and patriotic ideals. That was more than enough.[14]

This was the background of a revolutionary. A family that felt itself cut off from other privileged families by its consciousness of social inequalities. A personal temperament that was intelligent, mature, rebellious and stubborn. Travels over a continent where successions of bad governments had made mass poverty stink in the nostrils and shame the eyes. A doctor's concern for curing the incurable millions, whose diseases were only their symptoms, since the root case was social injustice. Personal experience of three failed revolutions – the Bolivian revolution, later to be overthrown by an army *putsch*; the Guatemalan revolution, destroyed by American intervention; and the Mexican revolution, rotted by internal sloth and decay. This experience changed a young doctor, whose nature was radical, into a revolutionary by intent. He had moved from passive indignation to active resistance, from observing to planning. His sympathy for suffering humanity had become a strategy for finding the remedy for that suffering. To become a total revolutionary, all Che needed was another revolution, which was at hand.

T W O

THE CUBAN WAR

The Cuban group of exiles led by Fidel Castro hardly reached a Mexican port, let alone Cuba. Castro was arrested by the Mexican intelligence services, along with Che Guevara and other supporters. Although Castro soon arranged for their release from prison through bribery and pressure from the Russian embassy, Che suffered his first experience of jail conditions and heard of the torture of his companions by beating and immersion in cold water. He asked Castro to leave him behind bars so that the Cuban revolution could continue. But Fidel said that he would not abandon his comrade, and he did not, securing Che's release in August 1956 to join him on the Rancho San Miguel near Chalco, where the rebels were being taught the basics of military training. Guevara led the squad in every exercise.

The expedition against the dictator Batista in Cuba was almost certain to fail. The eighty-two rebels who boarded the yacht *Granma* were badly trained, badly equipped and bad sailors. No one could navigate the boat properly, everybody was seasick, most of the supplies were jettisoned in a storm and the expedition landed in a mangrove swamp near the Sierra Maestra, a series of mountain chains in south-east Cuba. Their amateurishness in the first weeks of the guerrilla venture could almost have served as a manual of what not to do, just as Che's later book *Guerrilla Warfare* served as a manual of good practice. The early mistakes were often the lessons for their later successes. All strategists of guerrilla combat, including Che, stressed the same point, that the initial period was the most dangerous one, and that blunders and bad luck could annihilate the whole group at the outset.

Fidel Castro's force should have been destroyed on 5 December 1956 at the first battle at Alegría de Pío. A succession of fatal errors had led them into disaster. One of the few survivors, Universo Sánchez, told of how his feet were blistered by his new boots, of how their resting-place at Alegría de Pío was exposed to attack, of how they had allowed their guide to leave them and betray them to the nearby troops of Batista, of how ten aeroplanes circled overhead without the guerrillas thinking that they were particularly important, and of how they were resting with their weapons laid aside and their boots off. Batista's troops, far more professional than these untrained fighters, surrounded them and nearly wiped them out. The original group was reduced to a dozen men.

In his *Episodes of the Cuban Revolutionary War*, which he wrote from notes taken during the campaign, Che described his experiences with a great deal of irony, modesty and self-criticism. He found the early mistakes of the guerrillas 'both ridiculous and tragic'. He was wounded in the neck at Alegría de Pío and his reaction was touching and unsoldierly. Not unreasonably, he thought that he was dead, even though the wound did not turn out to be serious. His first concern was not to save his life – the primary duty of a guerrilla – but to die honourably:

> I immediately began to wonder what would be the best way to die, now that all seemed to be lost. I remembered an old story of Jack London's in which the hero, knowing that he is condemned to freeze to death in the icy wastes of Alaska, leans against a tree and decides to end his life with dignity. This is the only image I remember.[1]

Che's meditation on American literature was cut short by the curses of Juan Almeida, who forced him to run for his life. Later, Che was to be captured in Bolivia leaning against a tree, but that time he was wounded in the leg and unable to move, and he had run out of ammunition.

When Che fled with four of his surviving comrades, he made one important and symbolic choice between his duty as a doctor and as a revolutionary. 'This was perhaps the first time I was faced with the dilemma of choosing between my education for medicine and my duty as a revolutionary soldier. At my feet were a pack full of medicines and a cartridge box; together, they were too heavy to carry. I chose the cartridge box, leaving behind the medicine pack.'[2] Che had learned his first lesson as a guerrilla, that bullets matter more to a guerrilla's survival than even healing.

He was, however, to make more mistakes. He found himself with seven other comrades, groping his way towards the Sierra Maestra and a meeting-place with any other survivors. Drawing on his recollections of astronomy, he guided the group by the north star. Months later, he discovered that he had mistaken the north star for another star, and that their arrival in the right place was a matter of sheer luck. Afterwards, Che always carried a compass in his knapsack.

Surrounded by enemy patrols and starving, the eight men were totally dependent on help from the peasants of the Sierra Maestra. They were not disappointed. In one peasant's hut they feasted royally, and a constant procession of neighbours brought them gifts and sympathy. This early reception was to be cold comfort to Che in his last campaign in Bolivia, where after eight-and-a-half months of guerrilla activity, he would write of the Indian peasants there: 'They have to be hunted down to be made to talk, as they are just like little animals.'[3] Certainly without the help of the Cuban peasants, Che's little group would have been exterminated.

Yet the catalogue of early errors was not yet complete. Che's group decided to leave their guns, all their ammunition and their uniforms in the friendly peasant's hut, along with their one sick comrade 'as security'. They hoped to rejoin Fidel Castro more easily in the disguise of countrymen. Their host betrayed them, not intentionally, but from the peasant love of gossiping. Batista's men raided the hut, captured the sick man and seized all the weapons and supplies. When Che's group was led by the peasants to Fidel, their leader castigated them for their incompetence. Che recorded:

For the duration of the campaign and even today, his words remain engraved on my mind: 'You have not paid for the error you committed, because the price you pay for the abandonment of your weapons under such circumstances is your life. The one and only hope of survival that you would have had, in the event of a frontal clash with the Army, was your guns. To abandon them was criminal and stupid.'[4]

Later when Che was too ill to keep up with the group, he was also left in the care of a friendly peasant, but this time he was abandoned near the peasant's house without the peasant's wife even knowing that Che was there. He had learnt caution.

In the case of the few survivors of Alegría de Pío, survival was all. Five peasants joined them in the next month, and early in 1957 they made a successful attack on the La Plata barracks. Most of the rural population was still sitting on the fence and communications with potential rebels in the cities did not exist; but at least a beginning had been made. As Fidel declared, they now had twelve rifles and a victory to their credit, instead of only seven rifles and no victory at all. Even so, Che's mistakes continued. With rare vanity, he took to wearing a captured corporal's cap as a trophy from the victory. One day the cap was nearly shot from his head while he was out inspecting his own sentries, who naturally took him for an enemy.

The nucleus of the guerrilla force became acclimatized to life in the Sierra Maestra during the following months. There was one traitor among them, but the local population shielded them, although few joined the rebels. As Che was to find later in Bolivia, the hardest thing was to get new recruits. 'In that period, it was very difficult to enlarge our group; a few men came, but others left; the physical conditions of the struggle were very harsh, but the problems of morale even more so.'[5] This experience led Che to stress in *Guerrilla Warfare* how important it was never to risk or waste lives in the early stages, because these were literally irreplaceable.

The months in the Sierra Maestra taught the guerrillas their dependence on peasant support. The few countrymen who did actually join them were vital. They could always get food from their friends among the other peasants, they could pick the rural grapevine for news of enemy movements and they could teach urban recruits how to survive in the countryside. They were the real scouts and spies and foragers of the group. They helped to form a regional network of sympathizers, who could bring new recruits to the guerrilla band. As the successes and the legend of the 'bearded ones' grew, so peasant support increased. Castro began to establish a kind of extra-legal revolutionary state in a few villages, which also served as warning signals against an army attack.

Peasant support was based as much on calculation as idealism. Che's memoirs of the Cuban War are full of accounts of executions of rural informers, denounced by other peasants. The rebel force would protect its friends and neutrals and treat them fairly, but it was ruthless towards anyone who helped Batista's men. In many areas of the Sierra Maestra, it was eventually more dangerous to help the government than to help the rebels, in contrast to the later war in Bolivia, when Che was perpetually betrayed by Indians whom he could not control or terrorize into silence. In the Cuban War, however, Che noted of the peasants: 'Denouncing us did violence to their own conscience and, in any case, put them in danger, since revolutionary justice was speedy.'[6] He discovered a cold ruthlessness in his nature. Spilling blood was necessary for the cause. Within two years he would order the death of several hundred Batista partisans at La Cabaña, one of the mass killings of the Cuban Revolution. And after the failed Bay of Pigs invasion, all the captured Cuban exile leaders were shot.

Such contact with the peasants profoundly affected Che's whole theory of revolutionary strategy. Direct and personal experience in the Sierra Maestra informed one of the three fundamental statements with which he began *Guerrilla Warfare*: 'in the underdeveloped countries of the Americas, rural areas are the best battlefields for revolution.' Moreover, he insisted that 'the guerrilla makes agrarian reform his banner'. Che and his fellow Cuban revolutionaries emphasized later that they were not indebted to Mao Zedong's theories on peasant warfare, stressing they had not even read his writings or others of the same kind. Direct experience was always Che's best teacher.

One other lesson was learned in the early days of the war. Castro insisted on his troops behaving as humanely as possible towards wounded enemy soldiers, prisoners, civilians and peasants who did not collaborate with the enemy. The result was that the reputation of the guerrillas grew in contrast to the general brutalities practised by Batista's men. This was of practical help to Che himself, when he suffered from a bad bout of asthma. On one occasion his physical incapacity nearly had the whole Castro group liquidated. In the end he had to be left behind to recover in the care of peasants, who were won over by the guerrillas' humane policy. When Che tried to rejoin the group, he was so ill that he had to use his rifle as a crutch, and he took ten days to cross ground that he would normally have crossed in one.

Batista's cruelty in putting down a student plot in Havana brought new and essential help to the thirty men of the guerrilla force. A campaign of terror by the army in the Sierra Maestra had begun to shake the sympathy of the peasants, but now fifty new recruits from the cities joined the guerrillas. Thirty of them were armed, and in May 1957 a cargo of weapons was delivered to Castro's forces, including machine-guns, automatic rifles, carbines and 6,000 rounds of ammunition. Che and the veteran rebels were ecstatic at this strength, although disappointed at the poor quality of the new recruits, who soon distinguished themselves in the battle of El Uvero, in which Che himself played a major part. The 'nomadic phase' was nearly over. The growth of strength of the guerrilla forces made a vast difference to the attitude of Batista's army as well as to the morale of the guerrillas themselves. As Che noticed, 'There was a qualitative change. There was now a whole area which our enemies avoided for fear of meeting us, although we also showed little interest in bumping into them.'[7]

The 'nomadic phase' of the guerrillas in the Sierra Maestra had been a matter of kill or cure. Extremely incompetent at the beginning, the few survivors of Alegría de Pío soon became seasoned fighters. Partially disabled through ill health, Che never stopped his analysis of his own and the group's mistakes. Most of his later guerrilla theory – the setting up of a guerrilla focus, survival at all costs in the early days, the concentration on morale – was the direct outcome of his observations. Above all, he learned to appreciate the aid of the peasants, both as recruits and as suppliers for the guerrillas. Although the new recruits and the arms sent from the cities were usually vital, their help in the development of the guerrilla forces was later to be underestimated by Che for political reasons.

The triumph of El Uvero, when guerrillas successfully overwhelmed a small barracks in broad daylight by frontal assault, marked a change in the war. Batista's army withdrew from its outposts in the Sierra Maestra, leaving a large area to the rebels. From this time onwards, Che recalled, the enemy 'made only sporadic incursions into the Sierra. . . .

There was a true liberated zone. Precautionary measures were not so necessary. We were partially free to talk at night, to stir in our hammocks. Authorisation was given to move into the Sierra villages and establish a closer relationship with the people.'[8]

Yet success bred nearly as many problems as failure. The guerrilla forces had begun a period of continuous growth, which created new problems with food and supplies. The second phase of the Cuban War had started, with the guerrillas settled in semi-permanent encampments. There they set up service and supply sections, becoming a government in miniature. Small industries, radio stations and hospitals were established, laws were decreed, justice was administered through courts and an intensive campaign of indoctrination was set in motion. The state of armed truce with the Batista army even allowed the guerrillas to make deals with the peasants and village storekeepers for certain crops and supplies. The rebel forces had, to all intents and purposes, converted themselves into something approaching a regular army bivouacking in friendly territory.

Much of the credit for this organization must go to Che. His new-found planning skills date from this period. After the battle of El Uvero, he had been made a *Comandante*, the highest rank in the rebel forces, in charge of the Second Column, thus ranking directly beneath Castro himself. Batista's radio stations began to denounce him personally, along with the two Castro brothers. The journalist Enrique Meneses, who spent four months in the Sierra Maestra from December 1958, testified to Che's success in setting up a supply base for the guerrillas. On reaching Che's camp, he found a hospital housing twenty wounded men and two doctors, an armaments workshop, a tailor's shop making uniforms from olive-green cloth sent from Havana, a bakery and a printing machine, which produced a regular news-sheet. To Meneses the contrast between Fidel Castro and Che was evident. Fidel was the utopian dreamer, the speech-maker, always on the move, always planning. Che was the silent listener, who wanted a safe base for operations, the pragmatist who could carry out Fidel's dreams. Fidel and Che were interdependent, but already there were those who felt as much loyalty and admiration for Che as for their Cuban chief.

Yet this period of Che's life was not wholly devoted to the actions of the moment and winning the war in hand. He was also preoccupied with the general principles of all wars of liberation and with the new society to come in Cuba, once victory was won. A comrade, Rafael Chao, testified of Che at the time: 'He could be seen, sometimes very late, sitting on his hammock and writing down some notes. He also liked discussion very much. When everybody was already asleep, he would take a walk through camp, looking for someone who felt like having a talk.' He used to exchange letters with Raúl Castro, who still disagreed with many of his tenets of Marxism. And Che himself found that his growing clarity of vision helped his morale and that of all the guerrillas whom he influenced. 'Our leaders' and fighters' awareness was growing. The best among us felt deeply the need for an agrarian reform and an overturning of the social system, without which the country could never achieve health.'[9]

Fidel Castro had liaised with all the opposition parties in Cuba, promising them much in order to get their support against Batista. He had laid great hopes on a general strike, which was called in April 1958, in the cities. The failure of this manoeuvre proved more than a theoretical setback. It demoralized the opponents of Batista, cut off the lines of supply and communication between the cities and the Sierra Maestra, and led to an offensive by Batista's armies which aimed at wiping out the guerrillas during the summer. In point of fact, 320 rebels defeated 10,000 troops and spelled the end of the dictator. Yet Che's lack of faith in urban action to support guerrilla war can be traced back to these losses in the Cuban campaign. He never had much belief in the power of urban revolutionaries, whom he usually considered soft and unrealistic.

Che's own 'long march' through the island at the end of Castro's winning campaign in the autumn, which cut the island in two, confirmed his prejudices against the value of urban action. He liberated the towns from the mountains. He cut off communications between the cities, and thus isolated and finally seized Santa Clara and an armoured train. His own experience was of setting up a rural base, of expanding until towns fell into his hands, of isolating cities until they also fell. To Che the country had to liberate the city. Urban centres had to be conquered from without, not within. The Sierra campaign and the attitude of the Cuban Communist Party gave Che a strong bias against the Marxist–Leninist dogma of a rising led by the urban proletariat through a series of strikes, through sabotage and through a final revolt. The armed peasants could conquer the countryside until the cities tumbled like rotten bananas into their laps. This was the experience which was to lead Che into geographical isolation and death in Bolivia.

During his campaigning, Che had an affair with a beautiful mulatto woman, Zoila Rodríguez, and he met his future wife, Aleida March de la Torre, who came from as privileged a background as his own. A university student, she had been drawn into revolutionary politics and joined the guerrillas. Soon she became Che's inseparable companion. Intensely jealous and possessive, she would largely lose him to the international revolution just as Hilda Gadea had.

The twenty-five months of Che Guevara's early mistakes and successes as a guerrilla in the Sierra Maestra turned him into an organizer, a thinker, a tactical expert and something of a hero. Previously he had merely been a young, asthmatic and quixotic urban intellectual, who considered himself a revolutionary because of travel among the Latin American poor and a study of Marx and Lenin. He had been in no way different from thousands of other progressive middle-class Latin Americans in the liberal professions. Yet by the time that Fidel Castro's provisional government took over from Batista in January 1959, Che was a proven guerrilla fighter of great courage, power and ability. Now one of the leading figures in the new Cuba, he would soon be looked upon as the most important theorist of the revolution. His job was to put together 'in a systematic and coherent fashion' an ideology from the multitude of contradictory theories proliferating in Cuba in the wake of Castro's victory.

The Cuban War forged Che politically and ideologically. His contact with the peasants turned him into an 'agrarian revolutionary'. The near unanimity of the opposition to Batista's tyranny in the later stages of the struggle made him think in terms of a 'people's war'. The part played by the United States, which aided and supported Batista during most of the war, confirmed Che's hatred of 'Yankee imperialism'. The murky and opportunistic conduct of the politicians opposed to Batista, who allied themselves with Fidel Castro only for their own advantage, caused Che's disgust with the democratic procedure that threw up such connivers. Above all, the actual experience of beginning a war of liberation with a small group, which never grew to be as large as one army division, gave Che a set of unorthodox and non-Marxist ideas about guerrilla groups as the new 'flag-bearers' of the revolution.

Moreover, success depended, in Che's opinion, on the unquestioned leadership of a chief or *jefe maximo*, who was more important than a whole party organization of anonymous cadres. Publicity, indeed, was a condition of success for the small guerrilla group; fame rallied malcontents to the rebels' side. From his own experience of guerrilla warfare, Che applied maxims to cover most military strategy and the possibility of world revolution. Three recurrent themes in his *Episodes of the Cuban Revolutionary War* were the basis for all his future thinking.

First, actual combat was the best way of learning to be a guerrilla fighter. No amount of theory could make a good fighter. Only the experience of revolutionary war itself could sort out the true *guerrillero* from the dreamer or latent traitor.

Secondly, actual combat forged a believer as well as a fighter. A man might join the guerrilla group, totally ignorant of ideology. His social conscience as a revolutionary must develop hand in hand with his military skill, as military skill alone would never carry him through the hardships of a guerrilla war. Logically, therefore, the best fighter was also the most political man, and he was more fit than anyone else to become a leader after the war was won, being more realistic and revolutionary than anyone who had not fought.

Thirdly, the guerrilla group had its own mystique. Che's daily contact in the Sierra Maestra with a group of tough, courageous and idealistic men gave him a heroic concept of the *guerrillero*. The pages of his *Episodes* were full of tributes to the comrades he lost in the war. Che helped to create this legend of the revolutionary hero, even though this was against his ideas about equality. And when he himself died, he was to incarnate his own legend.

THREE

MASTER OF GUERRILLA WARFARE

Military experts might disagree with the political premisses which motivated Che Guevara, but they agree that his theories on guerrilla warfare were brilliant strategical studies. Che's writings on the subject were truly revolutionary. They outlined how a rising by a few men might win against the forces of modern armies and technology. Minimal resources, little initial popular support and poor communications were no reason not to begin an insurrection, which could pin down a regular army while gaining new recruits every day. Atom bombs were of little use in putting down jungle guerrillas; tanks could not operate in forests and mountains. The success of the Cuban attempt inflamed many others; its influence was global. From Vietnam to Afghanistan, Che's theories on guerrilla warfare held or defeated modern armies which were equipped to crush anything except this form of fighting.

For Che, guerrilla warfare was an early stage of classical warfare and could not, by itself, win a war. But it was the training ground which developed a nucleus of rebels into a small army capable of fighting pitched battles against the army of the oppressor. As each guerrilla was 'his own general,' it was his duty to protect his own life as carefully as a general did. Here Che made an interesting distinction between the ordinary soldier and the guerrilla fighter. 'Each guerrilla must be ready to die, not to defend an ideal, but to transform it into a reality.'[1]

As the regular army's aim was to destroy each and every guerrilla, the fighter's first aim was to discover the army's strategy and to thwart it. The defeat of that army was his strategy. His main supply of weapons would come from the army he fought, so that the enemy would help to destroy himself. Better, indeed, to use the same weapons, so that ammunition could be captured and used against the enemy. The whole guerrilla campaign should be planned in three phases that comprised: survival and adaptation to conditions of guerrilla life; erosion of enemy strength in the area marked out by the guerrilla group for its own territory; and attacks on the enemy on his own ground concentrating on communications and bases.

Che's rules for the campaign were emphatic. Strike the enemy constantly. Give him the impression that he is being harassed and encircled. Teach the local population the aims of the guerrilla band, so that the people can see their advantage in aiding the insurrection. Use sabotage to demoralize the enemy and paralyse him by cutting off his communications. Avoid useless acts of terrorism. Try not to hold too much territory. Create new guerrilla groups when sufficient recruits join. These new groups would hold more territory, until the offensive against the army on its own ground could start.

In all conditions, tactics must be adapted to circumstances. The guerrilla force must constantly improvise and transform all incidents to its own advantage. Classical war must be left to the enemy; the guerrillas must be unpredictable. Speed must characterize all assaults. 'The essential elements of the guerrilla group are surprise, deception, and night operations.' Ambushes and the use of mines would bring in most captured weapons. The guerrilla group must be 'implacable' in attack, also in treating murderers and torturers. But it must be merciful to enemy soldiers; it must free prisoners and care for the enemy wounded. It must also show great consideration for the civilian population and local customs. In this way, it would prove its *moral* superiority over the enemy.

Che's *Guerrilla Warfare* examined different strategies for fighting on favourable and unfavourable ground and urban areas. He discussed what types of arms should be used in each area, the requisite number of men and the tactics dictated by geography. Favourable ground was unsuitable for sabotage, capturing weapons and getting supplies. Unfavourable ground demanded a campaign of great mobility. Action in urban areas could only be part of an overall strategy and must be directed wholly from *outside* the cities. Che concluded this section of his book by stressing the primacy of the countryside as a base for all guerrilla operations. Urban risings should only take place when the war in the rural areas needed support.

In the second part of his work, Che developed his theme of the nature of the guerrilla and of the rebel group. The guerrilla's role as an agrarian reformer and as 'a crusader for the people's freedom' was further defined. Each guerrilla must show impeccable moral conduct and strict self-control.

'He must be an ascetic . . . and must always aid the peasant technically, economically, morally and culturally.' This behaviour anticipated the guerrilla's role after the war was won, when the reform of the social structure would become a natural continuation of the rebellion itself.

In the same way, the guerrilla anticipated his future control of the means of justice and law by punishing traitors, by expropriating surplus land and livestock to redistribute to the poorer peasants, and by confiscating the property and businesses of the enemies of the revolution. He must also try to establish cooperatives, if possible, and to indoctrinate the local population ideologically. At this stage, there would be an interaction between the guerrillas and the peasants. The guerrilla, who was often an educated man of middle-class origins, would use his superior learning to enlighten the peasants, while the peasants would show him the *reality* of their social condition, which the guerrilla had only known before in an abstract way. The peasants could also give a practical lesson to the guerrilla, teaching him what reforms were most needed.

Che then discussed the role of women in such a war. He first denounced the 'colonial mentality' of Latin Americans, who underestimated women to the point of discriminating against them. In fact, women made fine fighters and could also service the guerrilla group, acting as tailors, cooks and nurses. In civilian action they were important as teachers and, above all, as couriers, taking messages between rebel and government territory. The presence of women should not lead to sexual rivalry among the guerrillas. A woman with them should behave according to their moral education, although Che saw no reason why a revolutionary man and woman should not sleep together if they were 'in love and have no other commitments'. He had set such an example in the Sierra Maestra.

The role of the guerrilla doctor was particularly important to Che. Psychologically, especially in the early days of the group, the doctor was fundamental as a source of strength to the wounded and ill. Medicines were less important than comfort. 'For a man in pain, a simple aspirin takes on importance when it is administered by the friendly hand of somebody who feels and identifies with the man's suffering.' Che continued with technical descriptions of establishing elementary hospitals, the use of stretcher-bearers, the performance of operations in the field and the other functions of healing in war.

Che then dealt with propaganda, which he largely defined in terms of news reporting. Rebel newspapers and radio must tell the truth at all costs. The object of the revolutionary media must be to tell the facts of battles and growing strength, because the government media would certainly be lying. The social programme of the guerrillas must also be explained. Getting information about the enemy was another necessity; peasants often made bad informers, and women good ones.

Che went on to examine the training of recruits and the structure of the guerrilla force. Unlike the system in Latin American regular armies, promotion should only be given to men who deserved the rank and won it in combat. The guerrilla force could not succeed without a great leader, who gave it sufficient time for training in absolute secrecy. For a guerrilla force must not only defeat the army and overthrow the government; it must also defend power after the revolution is won. The regulars must be disbanded and a people's army created in their place, made up of peasants, workers and soldiers.

In the last chapter of *Guerrilla Warfare*, Che analysed the present and future situation in Cuba. He described what the Revolutionary Government had done since it came into power and demonstrated how these actions were the logical outcome of the war itself. Inevitably, these radical reforms had led to a break with the imperialist power which used to control Cuba, the United States, but Cuba no longer needed or feared the United States. No countries which liberated themselves should fear alienating past colonial or neo-colonial powers. Che described the sanctions and pressures exerted on Cuba by North American policy and denied that they could wreck the Cuban economy. Perhaps the United States might invade and inflict damage on the Cuban army, navy and air force, as would occur in the Bay of Pigs invasion by Cuban exiles. Yet the Revolution would survive such an attack, because it had kept its promises to the Cuban people who would defend it to the death. That prophecy turned out to be most true. When 1,500 well-equipped Cuban exiles later invaded (compared to the 82 people who came off the *Granma*), they were easily destroyed, making the Suez campaign, as the British ambassador wrote, 'look like a successful picnic'. This victory enabled Castro to consolidate his revolution.

Elsewhere, Che conceded that the Cuban Revolution had three special factors working in its favour: the leadership of Fidel Castro, the unpreparedness of the United States, and the class consciousness of the Cuban peasants who had suffered from the plantation system. Even so, Che maintained that the Cuban Revolution was no rare case. It could happen elsewhere. The basic factors were to be found in other underdeveloped or semi-developed countries. If one favourable factor was missing, another one would probably aid new guerrillas. The Cuban example was globally applicable.

Critics of *Guerrilla Warfare* called the book wise after the event, for it seemed to rationalize improvised responses to situations beyond Fidel Castro's control. Che never denied this criticism, for his analysis was the refinement of past success and failure. What he did deny was that the Cuban experience was unique and insular. The Cuban War might have been the basis for nearly all Che's theories, but he thought that most of the world could study and apply the Cuban experience.

There is no way to calculate whether Che or Fidel was the greater military leader. They were symbiotic. *Guerrilla Warfare* was a distillation of Che's original ideas and Fidel's strategy. They believed that revolutions could be started and won in almost every Latin American country, and that Fidel was speaking for all of them when he later said that the Cordillera of the Andes had to be turned into the Sierra Maestra of South America. Che sought to demonstrate that this was feasible by writing a manual and by fighting later in Bolivia.

Frequent comparisons were made between Mao Zedong's and Che Guevara's theories of guerrilla war. The primacy of guerrilla methods and of the countryside as the area of operations was common to both. Yet Che and other Cuban revolutionaries always insisted that they won their war against Batista without knowledge of the Chinese experience. This was probably true, even if the Cubans were bound to stress the particular nature of their rising. There were enough parallels between the Cuban and the Chinese situations to assume that their leaders would have drawn similar conclusions. Both insurrections began in the cities, where they failed to get enough support and lost to the regular army in actual combat. Both subsequently continued in rural areas, where they gained local backing and began to defeat the regular army. Both made agrarian reform their chief revolutionary pledge, putting the peasants in the place of the urban proletariat as the new revolutionary class.

The fact that the Cuban revolutionaries won *without* the support of the Cuban Communist Party, and the fact that they won long before they themselves turned to Communism as an ideology, accounted for the chief unorthodoxy of Che's writings in *Guerrilla Warfare*. Even the Chinese had never dared to put forward such a heresy. For Che's Cuban experience made him preach the autonomy of the guerrilla group *outside* the central control of the monolithic Communist parties, usually based in the cities. The leaders of the Communist Party of Cuba had not risked everything, nor had the political exiles, nor the democratic groups which opposed Batista. Therefore, they did not deserve to lead the new Cuba. They only deserved to serve under those who had actually won the victory with their blood and sweat and sacrifice.

FOUR

The Changing Revolution

In January 1959 Fidel Castro set the task of the young revolutionaries who entered Havana with him. When he had been released from jail by Batista five years previously, he had declared: 'Our freedom will not be a fiesta or a rest, but a struggle and a duty . . .' Most of Fidel's comrades were ill-equipped for the struggle and the duty of administering a country; Che was one of the few exceptions. Even if he had no practical experience of economic policy, diplomacy or administration, he was an educated and philo-sophical man, who had already shown managerial skills in the Sierra Maestra – unlike the courageous but nearly illiterate heroes, Juan Almeida and Camilo Cienfuegos. Yet Che's actual jobs within the Castro government were to be less important than the lessons which he learned from them and applied within them. Just as he had been the theoretician of the war, so he provided the dialectic of the government.

Unquestionably, Che Guevara contributed to the Cuban Revolution almost as much as Fidel Castro did. Without Che's observant analysis and occasional eloquence, shown in such pieces as his important *Man and Socialism in Cuba*, the insurrection would have lacked both definition and vision. Fidel was a lawyer and a leader. For him, the laws and the pleas and the set speeches of prosecution and defence, with the people as the jury. But Che was a doctor. For him, the diagnosis and the cure, the meaning of life and death.

The relative positions of Fidel and Che within Cuba also dictated different attitudes. As the *jefe maximo*, Fidel had to keep the Revolution going and the economy of the island above water. He had to make the political deals necessary for internal security and external loans. He had to balance the conflicting forces among his followers and to listen to the wishes and complaints of the Cuban people. He had to bluff and trade for Russian support, and avoid provoking the United States to the point of intervention. His preoccupations were with the daily business of running a country.

While Fidel dealt with the problems as they arose, both in the Sierra Maestra and later in Havana, his subordinate Che could concentrate on finding a theory for what he thought had to be done. The testimony of reporters made it plain that Fidel Castro did not foresee the shape of his future government while he was still fighting in the mountains. As the American correspondent Herbert Matthews wrote: 'Fidel naïvely (to use his own word to me) believed that the rebels could make a radical social revolution democratically. Since his basic aim was revolution, and democracy was simply the method that he thought he could use, when the crunch came he changed his method, not his goal.'[1] As Che was always the extremist on the left of the guerrilla leaders, Fidel's break with the democratic process and supposed 'betrayal' of the aims of the Revolution was partially the result of the *jefe maximo* taking Che's advice.

In the first year of the Revolution Fidel and his movement helped to set up a government of moderate middle-aged men with a record of integrity and opposition to Batista. This liberal group immediately began to clash with the more radical group of guerrilla leaders, who felt that they had many promises to keep to the Cuban peasants, and that radical reform demanded draconian measures. Soon Fidel squeezed out all the moderates and replaced them with comrades from the Sierra

Maestra. As Celia Sánchez testified, the rebels had thought they would have to govern through the liberals, but they found out that they were the masters of the island. At that moment, Che's concept of guerrilla government made sense. The opportunity chose its theory. If radical changes were to be made, only the guerrilla leaders could make them.

The six years Che spent in Cuba after 1959 encapsulate a history of the Cuban Revolution. When Jean-Paul Sartre called Che 'the most complete man of his age,' he was stating that Che lived his own words so fully that his own history and society told much the same story. The complexity of the Cuban Revolution, its dedication and its originality, its experiments and its failures, served as a dark mirror to Che Guevara. While he was helping to fashion the Revolution, the Revolution was helping to fashion him. Yet in six areas, Che's writing and practice were essential for the Cuban experiment – in agriculture, industry, monetary policy, moral incentives, revolutionary conscience and international affairs.

Cuba was mainly an agrarian society. Thus the Cuban Revolution had to be mainly an agrarian revolution. The economy of the island, as well as the emotion of the fighters from the Sierra Maestra, dictated the policy that the countryside came first.

Three-quarters of Cuba's foreign earnings came from
the sale of sugar alone. The cane harvest was the
condition of Cuban prosperity. Yet the landless
labourers who brought in the sugar were treated
worse than cattle, while the urban workers were
relatively privileged. The revolution needed the
support and the work of the peasants. Commem-
oration of the mountain war and Che's glorification
of the rural workers as *the* revolutionary class were
merely the sentiments behind a political need.
Agrarian reform had already been started in the areas
taken by the rebels. Now they held the whole island,
that reform should encompass all of the country.

The most important law issued by the new
revolutionary government was the First Agrarian
Reform of May 1959. The plantations, large farms
and major properties were all nationalized. Emphasis
was placed on moving from a one-crop economy to
diversity in agriculture. Full employment all the year
round was the aim. Cooperative and state farms
were set up as examples, while small farmers, who
still kept their land, were given credits and were
taught improved methods of cultivation. Che had
preferred to emphasize the role of the peasants as a
class; and now agrarian reform ushered in the
concept of a class struggle. It divided Cuban

society into two camps: on the one side, the landowners; on the other side, the peasants, now supported by the urban workers.

These events coincided with the inclination of the Cuban leaders towards Marxism–Leninism, with their rapprochement with the Cuban Communist Party, with their worsening relationship with the United States after the nationalization of North American-owned plantations, and with their new friendship with the Soviet Union, delighted to extend its influence so close to the shores of Florida. Moreover, the urban workers were beginning to realize that they might also benefit from this rural revolution, while the middle class was increasingly alienated by Fidel's break with the old democratic leaders and with the United States, long the chief influence on Cuban diplomacy.

In this shift of government policy, Che was the instigator and theorist. The policy reflected the evolution in his thinking that had begun in Guatemala, had developed in Mexico City, and had formed in the Sierra Maestra. The revolutionary war against Batista and his tyranny had, for a time, made him concentrate his hate against a personal enemy and his henchmen. Despotism had a particular face. But soon after the victory Che turned his back on this feud. Foreign imperialism again became the real enemy, as it had been in Guatemala. The only lasting solution to the problems of underdeveloped countries, their only defiance against the economic power of imperialism, seemed to lie more in the creation of industries than in the development of agriculture, however just the distribution of land might seem to the poor agricultural labourer.

Soon the emphasis in Che's speeches began to alter. There was less said about the peasants, more about the urban workers; less said about land reform, more about new factories. By October 1959 Che was head of the industrial department of reorganization; then, after serving as Governor of the National Bank, he was made the Minister of Industry in February 1961. His early function was to oversee the conversion of agricultural products and wastes into raw materials; his later function was to spawn new processes to make Cuba self-sufficient. Underdevelopment became his bogey.

Che did not feel that he was deserting the peasants in his new emphasis on the workers of the cities. The field labourers were to be rewarded with land reform, social benefits, full employment, education, mechanization and crop diversification. Yet now only one class could free Cuba from its

Fidel Castro planning a campaign in the Sierra Maestra, with Che, Calixto
Garcia, Ramiro Valdés and Juan Almeida.

Fidel Castro and Che Guevara in the Sierra Maestra.

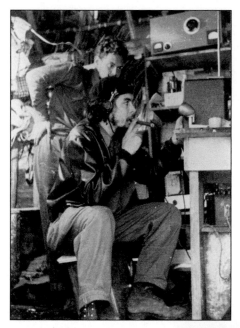

Che during the campaign of Las Villas at the Rebel Radio Station in the Escambray.

Che at the time of the battle of Santa Clara. On the left is Aleida March, whom he married in June 1959.

Che speaking to the Cuban people.

Che doing voluntary labour during
the sugar-cane harvest.

Che visiting China, November 1960.

Che with Jean-Paul Sartre and Simone de Beauvoir during their visit to
Cuba, 1965.

Che playing chess, one of his
favourite games.

Che with his parents, Celia de la Serna and Ernesto Guevara Lynch.

Che inspecting a mine while Minister of Industry.

Che in a Havana bus known as a *gua-gua*.

Che was the leader of a guerrilla
band in Bolivia until his death in
October 1967.

Fidel Castro announcing to the people of Cuba that he is convinced that the
murdered guerrilla leader known as Ramón is in fact Che Guevara,
10 October 1967.

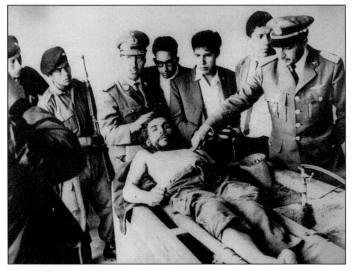

Bolivian officers, soldiers and journalists in the town of Vallegrande,
inspecting the dead body of Che Guevara.

underdevelopment, the urban workers. It was their turn to become the 'vanguard class' of the Revolution. And a new war had to be declared on the liberals and the middle classes.

Here Che revealed openly how much the example of the original Spanish *conquistadores* had mattered to the dozen guerrillas who had survived to conquer a whole island, just as Pizarro had survived with thirteen men on the Isle of Gallo before conquering the whole of Peru. Pizarro had drawn a line in the sand, over which only a handful had stepped, while the rest of his force had turned back in defeatism and despair. Yet Pizarro's small group had endured to win Peru, just as Fidel's group had gone on to win Cuba. And now the example of the great *conquistador* of the Incas was conjured up by Che to explain his attack on what he saw as the new enemies of the Revolution.

> Cuba has drawn the line in the sand again, and again we see Pizarro's dilemma: on the one hand, there are those who love the people, and on the other, those who hate the people. Between them, each time a bit more explicitly, the line divides the two great social forces, the *bourgeoisie* and the working class, which are defining with increasing clarity their respective positions as the process of the Cuban Revolution advances.[2]

As always, Che dated his preoccupation with new industries back to the experiences in the Sierra Maestra. He declared, 'Fidel remembered how in the Sierra we had once set up a small shoe factory, and from that time we became industrialists.' The setting up of industries was now part of the guerrilla struggle and of the global fight for the liberation of the Third World. 'Cuba's great impact has been as a political force – as the embodiment of all underdeveloped countries struggling for their freedom. The two elements of revolution are interrelated – the goal of those countries fighting for their freedom is to become industrialised in order to gain that freedom.' For the Third World, the guerrilla struggle was only the prelude to the industrial struggle against economic imperialism.

Naturally, that struggle demanded of the Cuban worker many of the qualities necessary for the guerrilla. Those in the factories had to acquire the same dedication and spirit of self-sacrifice that the rural fighters had possessed. The peasants had fought and won the first stage of the Revolution. Thus they were receiving their reward, the right use of the land. Now the city workers had to fight the second stage of the Revolution, the creation of a home industrial base. While this was being done, they must sacrifice many of the economic benefits which they already had, particularly the wages which gave them a standard of living many times higher than that of the rural labourer. They must not see in the new state merely another boss and a stingier boss. As their standard of living was bound to drop before it improved again, the workers had to identify their hopes for a prosperous future for themselves and their children with the success of the Revolution. And they had better do so gladly, in order to make their sacrifices worthwhile.

Foreign critics of Guevara found his switch of emphasis most cynical. When he needed the support of the peasants, he called for their self-denial and backed agrarian reform. But when he needed the urban workers more than the peasants, he called for their self-denial in the name of industrial growth. During the first stage, hatred of the landowners forged a bond between the guerrillas and the peasants; during the second stage, the bourgeoisie was attacked in order to appease the workers. In both cases, the theory and the ideology seemed to be justifications of *Realpolitik*; for instance, the local Communist Party was courted when its strength in the labour unions was needed to keep the urban workers from striking. Che appeared merely to be adding a gloss of concept to a smart strategy worthy of any politician.

Yet experience and analysis, practice and plan were inextricably connected. Che's political progress and that of Cuba kept pace during the first years of revolutionary government. The interaction between Che's ideology and public policy was almost a marriage of aims, as well as of convenience. In those decades, well before the collapse of the Soviet empire, the vocabulary of Marxism was universally accepted in the Eastern bloc of socialist nations. Terms such as 'working class' and *bourgeoisie* appeared to be accurate descriptions of social groups and economic categories. And though Russia held a larger empire than America through the military power of the Red Army, 'imperialism' was the evil policy of capitalist countries alone.

Before the triumph of democracy and market economics over Marxism, and until the collapse of the Soviet empire, the economic and social policies of Che Guevara would have appeared logical and necessary for an undeveloped country. Unfortunately, his theory and ideology applied better to the age before the Second World War than to his own. Even the Russians tried to dissuade Che from his grandiose plans to industrialize Cuba and double the standard of living on the island within five years. Yet as always, his hopes and radical views outstripped the arts of the possible and the practical. If a dozen men had conquered a country so quickly, surely an economy could be transformed in as short a time. It was not to be and could not be.

FIVE

AN END TO MONEY

Both in theory and in practice, Che Guevara despised money. His personal life had always been a reproach to greed. He lived in a spartan house in Havana. Even though his new wife Aleida bore him two sons, Camilo and Ernesto, and two daughters, Aleidita and Celia, he allowed his family few luxuries. He gave the many expensive personal gifts from other socialist régimes to training schools in Cuba. His only concession to himself was to smoke hand-rolled cigars. He seemed to get as much satisfaction from doing without money as most individuals get from spending it. His personal asceticism led him to a primitive communism in which money was an unnecessary evil.

He loathed cash as a medieval monk loathed usury. From his youth, his scorn was chiefly reserved for those who spent their whole time in piling up a fortune. In his farewell letter to Fidel, there would be a quiet pride in his assertion: 'I have left no material possessions to my wife and children, and I do not regret it. I am happy that it is this way.'[1] To most men, this admission would be humiliating; to Che, it was a source of strength. How many other Latin American politicians could say the same on leaving office? And how many of them had worked for a government thought to be so just that they need not worry about the future of a wife left with four small children to support?

Che was opposed not only to greed in individuals, but also in enterprises and nations. He hated the principle of foreign loans; he thought they should be gifts. Such sentiments not only made Che the sworn enemy of capitalism and a free market, but also led him to oppose many practices of the Soviet bloc, particularly Russia's loans at interest to Cuba. He was outraged by the fact that, in most societies, workers had to sell their labour and skills to the highest bidder. He could never accept that human beings or nations should be motivated by greed, so he opposed the method of material incentives to increase productivity, and also the harsh workings of the law of supply and demand. He dreamed of the single wage-scale, in which everybody would earn the same amount or would earn according to his needs, until money could be abolished altogether. Public demand for a certain product or skill should not pay more for it than for another, less popular but socially more desirable.

Ironically enough this arch-enemy of money was chosen to run the National Bank of Cuba, before he became Minister of Industry. Yet there was a perverse logic in the choice of Che. To fight prostitution, a reformer goes to the brothel, not to the home of a virtuous woman. To fight the old monetary system, a man becomes director of the national bank. Che's special concern with industrialization in Cuba must also have had something to do with his decision. He had to get the loans and credits and subsidies to finance his projects for new factories and processes. Like Brecht's Good Woman of Setzuan, Che had to put on the mask of the wicked financier in order to keep the wheels of industry turning. With Macheath in another Brecht play, *The Threepenny Opera*, he could have pondered: 'What is robbing a bank compared with running a bank?'

Before he took on his new job, Che had no more than an intelligent man's knowledge of economics. So he quickly educated himself in banking theory. He wrote many articles on finance, quoting Marxist and Hegelian sources to refute orthodox Communist and capitalist economists who defended or worked with the world's monetary system. Che's morals fundamentally dictated his economic theories; his learning was window-dressing. Although he taught himself the methods of banking, he wanted to use finance merely as a weapon to impose his ideology. To prove his beliefs, the methods had to work. But the reasons for choosing one method rather than another were not economic; they were moral. Che's vision of the new Socialist Man was never far from his thoughts on revolution, warfare or economics. He was striving to create that new being and to end man's exploitation by man. Everything, including economics, had to serve the birth of those ideals. Here lay Che's originality and influence.

Che believed that a fresh socialist government inherited a great many capitalist ways of thought alien to the purpose of the revolution. These ways had to be blotted out at once, or they would corrupt the new comradeship and radicalism. It was not enough to turn the old system into a welfare state, to nationalize industries and to distribute wealth more justly. Marxism and central planning were more than a means to run a state more efficiently and fairly. Unless the new system could alter the relationship of men to one another and to their society, then all the struggle and suffering of the rebellion against the previous régime was not worth the dead and the maimed and the losses. Moreover, there would be another rebellion, if the new system was merely an improved model of the bad old ways.

For socialism to mean more than a higher standard of living for an exploited majority, the quality of life had to be bettered. A significance for living had to be provided along with material advance. Above all, that meaning had to apply to man's labour. Socialism had to supply 'a future in which work will be man's greatest dignity, in which work will be a social duty as well as a true human pleasure and the ultimate act of creation'.[2] While a man's labour was a mere commodity to be bought and sold, he could not see his work in these terms. It was 'a sad duty, an unfortunate necessity'. That was the true curse of capitalism: it alienated man from what should be the source of his greatest satisfaction, pride in his labour. By changing his pride in work well done to a quest for the cash rewards for output, capitalism had corrupted the dignity of the worker and had turned him into a greedy parody of himself, where he laboured for what he could buy in his leisure time, not for the job itself. Change the worker's attitude towards his work and towards his rewards, and then the economy and the society and the man would change towards true socialism.

Che felt that this problem had to be dealt with at once during the first fervour of revolutionary pride. He clashed here with the old-line Communists. They wanted to set up a socialist economy first of all; when it was successful, then a true socialist mentality would develop in the workers. Che disagreed. After fifty years of socialism in Soviet Russia, too many capitalist incentives and ways of thought still remained among workers and managers. Indoctrination should precede rewards for increased production. 'We affirm that, in a relatively short time, the development of conscience does more for the development of production than material incentives.' The development of conscience meant getting workers to toil by appealing not to their greed or to their ambition or to their fear, but to their idealism and to their belief in their leaders and to their longing for a better future for their whole community as well as for themselves. With the state looking after their every need, the workers could labour for the good of all, until money became as obsolete as slavery.

Che's Theory of Value, which Fidel supported, was the basis of the whole economic argument.

Value was not defined according to supply and demand. It was defined according to the moral and social worth of a product or service, not its worth on the market. Thus the value of work was more important in human terms than in terms of economic efficiency. The state bank should calculate the budget for enterprises according to their social value, not give loans to state monopolies run by managers obsessed by mere productivity, as in Russia. Che thought of value in its old moral sense, not its narrow economic definition. Economic man was a monster created by the capitalist system; man was the social and political being defined by the ancient Greek philosophers. The economic system should serve man's values by serving the values of his society. Money was worth no part of a man's life.

This utopian Theory of Value governed Che's decisions as Governor of the National Bank. He thought it unfair to encourage competition between a state enterprise that manufactured beer and one that manufactured textbooks, just because the beer sold far better than the textbooks. To expand the beer industry because it was profitable was socially undesirable, if it meant less money to produce textbooks. The duty of the National Bank was to judge the relative value of the two products to

Cuban society, and then to allot a budget to each enterprise, determined by the social value of the product rather than by the profit made by the Cuban state. Loans to industries were to be free of interest, to prevent any pressure being put on the industry which might corrupt its social purpose in the quest for profits. In the same way, workers must not be given a share of the industrial profits; otherwise, a class of privileged workers would be created who would earn more than other workers who benefited the whole community by labour in unprofitable enterprises. The reward of labour was the good of all. The National Bank must discourage undue competition and incentives, the twin brothers of greed. Its decisions must teach the only true value, comradeship in the service of the Revolution.

These beliefs led Che to make difficult choices on the question of centralized planning. Obviously, local planning led to a greater feeling of participation, but it also allowed competition among various areas. Central planning allowed the organization of the whole island; it also aided the introduction of better technology and processes. In one of his speeches defending the idea of concentrated control, Che called capitalist competition 'a struggle among beasts' and socialist competition aiming at maximum profits 'a struggle among caged beasts'. Che would never be pragmatic over economic theory; he would rather be fanatic. He was after the fulfilment of human yearning; bodily needs were incidental. Even over such a socialist matter as voluntary labour, Che wanted more than the work itself. 'Volunteer work is not only a factor to augment production; it is the fountainhead of socialist education for the masses.'[3]

Thus Che and his school of economists wanted central planning, with all profits returning to the state for distribution over the entire economy and society. Agriculture should be run in the same way as industry; huge state farms should employ all labourers permanently on a salary, and profits should be ploughed back into the collective. The dominant goal should be industrialization as the only method of emancipating Cuba from a world market in which the developed powers bought raw materials at low cost and sold finished goods at high cost. Industrialization was also the only cure for the unemployment that plagued all underdeveloped countries. Agrarian reform was essential as well, in order to move a poor country from a one-crop economy to self-sufficiency, even if this meant cutting down the basic crop which provided foreign capital. Economic independence was the basis of political independence.

The motive behind this programme was to be supplied by revolutionary consciousness. 'The construction of socialism is not work alone. The construction of socialism is not consciousness alone. It is work and consciousness, development of material goods through work and development of consciousness.' But the development of a revolutionary consciousness must be more important than the development of production. For instance, although competition was bad in capitalist or socialist states when it encouraged rivalry and material differences, it was good when it encouraged true comrades to work harder, though it was a double-edged sword. 'Competition cannot be like a ball-game where the loser throws oranges at the referee. Competition should be fraternal. Why? So that every one produces more. It is a weapon to increase production. Not only that, it is also an instrument to deepen the consciousness of the masses, and the two must always go together.'[4] The same distinction applied to voluntary labour, which was a form of education in which work ceased to be an obsession, as in the capitalist world, and became a pleasant social duty. The making of a new man was the prime aim of all social tasks.

Yet Che was not completely dogmatic or rigid in his thinking, even with all his emphasis on central planning. He did not want to build a powerful state, but a happy socialist people. In fact, he denounced those who thought in orthodox and set terms. 'The task of creating a socialist society in Cuba must be met by fleeing mechanical thinking like the plague; mechanical thinking only leads to stereotyped methods.' Marxism was a dialectic, a process of change. Sectarianism within Marxism was a disease, a refusal to experiment. To Che, the revolutionary had to remain a human being. 'Being human' meant the opposite of being weak or behaving no better than most other humans. It meant acting for the best rather than for the least effort. Above all, it meant that a man should develop his sensibility, so that 'he feels anguish when a man is assassinated in any corner of the world, and he feels elation when in some corner of the world a new banner of liberty is raised'. Che found the words 'human' and 'revolutionary' the same. That was the conscience of the revolutionary.

There is no question that Che's economic theories contained an element of contradiction. A streak of utopian anarchism and primitive Communism lay at the back of all his emphasis on central control. At one workers' rally, Che began his speech by quoting a poet in exile who was lamenting that nobody had been able 'to dig the rhythm of the sun' or 'to cut an ear of corn with love and grace'. Che then explained that the Cubans had left this sort of attitude behind them and had created a new one through their desire 'to return to nature, to change daily chores into meaningful play'. If the poet came back to Cuba, he would see 'how man, after passing through all the stages of capitalist alienation, and after being thought a beast of burden in harness to the yoke of the exploiter, has found his way back again to play. In Cuba today, work takes on a new meaning. It is done with a new happiness.'[5] Che went on to stress there was, indeed, 'love and grace' in the very action of cutting sugar cane, and that the slavery of man did not lie in his need to work, but in his failure to own the means of production. When man repossessed the means of production, he also regained his old sense of happiness in work. He felt himself important within the social mechanism.

Ironically enough, Che revealed himself in this speech to be near the position of the original Puritan ethic which was the motor for the North American economy. The Puritans had always stressed that work was a social duty and should be joyfully performed. As Herbert's hymn pointed out, the man

> Who sweeps a room as for Thy laws
> Makes that and the action fine.

The laws of Che's society were not those of a seventeenth-century society, but the methods of persuading men to work hard and happily at menial jobs were no different.

In his famous essay, *Man and Socialism in Cuba*, Che summed up his economic philosophy. He began by denying that the Cuban state was setting out to extinguish the individual. It was setting out to create a new individual, glimpsed in the days of heroic fighting in the Sierra Maestra and when the whole population had sacrificed itself to serve the nation during the 1962 Missile Crisis and during Hurricane Flora. The people had served their country well: only the weather had failed them and Krushchev had backed down, restoring the prestige of the American after the Bay of Pigs disaster. The problem was to perpetuate the sense of service that emerged during days of crisis or disaster. That sense depended on perfect communications between the people and its leaders. 'The initiative generally comes from Fidel or the high command of the Revolution; it is explained to the people, who make it their own. At times local experiences are taken up by the party and the government and are thus generalized.' These communications were not yet good enough, which explained certain failures in understanding; but they would improve.

Of course, such a system of government appeared to mean the subordination of the individual. Yet to Che, Western individualism meant no more than the rule of capitalism. To him, Rockefeller was the supreme individualist of the West. 'It is a race of wolves. He who arrives does so only at the expense of the failure of others.' In socialism the individual was not a greedy being, but an unfinished product. Socialist society had to eradicate flaws of bad conditioning from the individual and the individual had to re-educate himself. He had to forget the twin ideas of capitalism – that the individual is isolated, and that relationships are governed by the law of supply and demand. To build revolutionary consciousness, a new man had to be created simultaneously with a new material base for the nation.

Thus the new society had to be a huge school, and, indeed, the Revolution had brought literacy to the masses. Capitalism might resort to force, but it also educated its people in the meaning of its system. The Cuban government had to indoctrinate its people even more intensively, because they had to unlearn the errors of capitalism. Only then could a new sort of man begin to emerge. His image was unfinished and would never be complete, because he was advancing parallel to the development of fresh economic forms. He no longer progressed *alone* towards vague personal longings. With the masses, he followed his party leaders towards the goals of the new society. He supported revolutionary institutions and sacrifices, but even they were only transitory stages towards the remade world. The ultimate goal of the Revolution was to set men free from their alienation from their society, which they miscalled their individualism. 'In spite of the apparent standardisation of man in socialism, he is more complete.'

Thus Che ignored the question of how the individual can oppose his society by stating that it was not a real question. The censorship now imposed on the free press in Cuba needed no excuse. Che agreed with Plato in saying that the realization of each man lay within his communistic society. Thus each man's voice must be heard *within* the social apparatus, not against it. All divisive tendencies that turned comrades into rivals must go – work for money, undue competition. Labour must be a social duty, leaving time for the enrichment of society by other pursuits. 'The machine is only the front line where duty is performed.' Freed from having to work in order to feed, clothe and house his family, a man could see himself fulfilled in his work for the whole community. Che admitted that work in the socialist state still had to be partly coercive, but that pressure should be what Fidel called 'moral compulsion', which would wither away when social conscience developed properly and generally.

Che thought that art really showed the difference between the capitalist and the socialist society. In capitalism, the artist attacked the state. 'Senseless anguish and vulgar pastimes are comfortable safety-valves for human uneasiness.' Yet the true revolution contained all artistic experimentation within itself. Admittedly there were 'no artists of great authority who also have great revolutionary authority'. Yet the Revolution was still young and experiment would discover them and the new socialist man. Che scorned the social realism of the nineteenth century, which was enshrined as the official art of Soviet Russia and China. That was reactionary, just as Western decadent art of the twentieth century was a reaction in itself to that outdated realism. Bold and persistent experiments would find a new art fit for revolutionary man. So again Guevara stood against the millennia of individual and global artistic expression in the absurd hope of creating some original and Cuban art forms that could and would never emerge.

For Che, even the future artist would find his inspiration in the guerrilla leaders of the Cuban Revolution, particularly in their self-sacrifice. They were guided by authentic feelings of love, yet they had given up their family life for the cause. 'There is no life outside the Revolution.' The people must follow their leaders' example towards true proletarian internationalism, a longing to help their exploited comrades all over the world. The leaders must educate the masses towards this end. 'We are at the head of the people that is at the head of America.'[6]

Che's early hopes and exaggerated intentions were bound to be disappointed. Even in Cuba, utopia was not just around the corner. In an article written in October 1964 Che analysed the errors made by the government in agriculture and in industry. An expert at self-criticism, Che judged his country's and his own mistakes as harshly and as lucidly as any enemy could have done. He had attacked the one-crop system as the bane of underdeveloped countries, and he had supported diversification in agriculture as the means to full rural employment and national self-sufficiency. Theoretically correct, in practice the policy had been a failure. Too much diversification was attempted at once; there was a general decline in agricultural production. Thus Cuba had to return to its original role as a major producer of sugar, the basic economic fact of its existence. Che now conceded that the belief which connected sugar with Cuba's dependence on imperialism and with misery in rural areas had been only a fetish. The truth was that the Cubans should produce sugar and get more money for it. The cane crop was not the devil; the balance of trade was.

Similar errors had taken place in Cuba's immediate and enthusiastic industrialization. Che admitted to a failure in understanding the precise technology and economics necessary in setting up new industries. Again, unemployment and a wish for national self-sufficiency had made the Cubans acquire too many factories too fast. The result was that these produced shoddy consumer goods at a high price by international standards. Even the problem of paying for imported consumer goods was not much helped, because the cost of importing raw materials was almost as high. Sadly, and expensively, the new Cuban government had to learn the gap between ideology and practice, between Marxism and the market.

An obsession with the need to industrialize and a determination to manufacture consumer goods at

home rather than to import them were under-
standable errors for Cuba to make. After all, in
Batista's time the United States had bought nearly
all Cuba's sugar and had supplied nearly all Cuba's
goods. Now the United States had become Cuba's
enemy and its past policy was anathema to Che. The
North American economic blockade of the island,
which effectively reduced the flow of Western
goods to a trickle, had made Cuba dependent on
supplies from the Eastern bloc several thousand miles
away – hardly a good argument for refusing to try to
make goods at home. The logic of past and present
trading difficulties, just as much as ideology, had
forced Cuba to experiment with home production,
even though the policy was doomed to fail.

Che also confessed to theoretical errors in
economic planning. These errors were of two
contradictory kinds. One series of errors came from
imitating the Russian Five Year Plans with their rigid
stages of decision and unattainable production
norms. The other series of errors sprang from snap
decisions, made on the spot to push everything
forward faster than it could go. These errors were
aggravated by other factors: the shortage of spare
parts for machinery that originally came from the
United States, the irregular supplies of new

machinery sent by the friendly nations in the Eastern
bloc, the mass exodus of bourgeois managers and
technicians, the lack of statistical and expert
knowledge, and the priority given to expropriation
and redistribution of wealth during the first few years
of revolution. A new world at home was not to be
had in a hurry. Only in revolutions abroad could
there be quick and deep change.

IN SEARCH OF LIBERATION

The life of a guerrilla fighter makes all other lives unsatisfactory. Just as Tom in *The Great Gatsby* was always seeking the dramatic turbulence of some irrecoverable football game, so Che sat behind his desk, always seeking the charged days of the Sierra Maestra. In war Che found his kind of peace. In liberating others, he liberated himself.

From 1960 onwards, Che had often served as a roving ambassador for Fidel Castro; he had been on important missions to Moscow — largely unsuccessful — to North Vietnam and Algeria, and to other Communist and non-aligned countries. But when Che left Cuba in 1965 to become a permanent wandering fighter round the world, he was acting out his creed that the duty of the Cuban Revolution was to help other countries to fight against imperialism. And there were other reasons. Che's relationship with Fidel, while comradely and admiring, was a difficult one. The Cuban Revolution totally engaged Fidel, while Che remained preoccupied with extending the war to Latin America and to the whole world.

Fidel could be a permanent revolutionary within the Cuban Revolution; Che could only be a permanent revolutionary outside it. Fidel was the leader in Cuba; Che wanted to be the leader elsewhere. Fidel had won the Cuban Revolution; Che wanted to win other revolutions. Fidel was a natural and brilliant politician; Che was a natural and brilliant crusader. Fidel found satisfaction in national planning and diplomacy and speech-making; Che was bored by deals and words alone. Moreover, Fidel was a supporter of a close alliance with Russia, which was falling out with the fellow Communist power of China, whereas Che preferred the latter régime's policies. In addition, Fidel had found out that Che's economic ideas did not work immediately, and Che did not like a sense of failure. Fidel would offer the best 5,000 sugar-cane cutters glittering prizes, which put paid to Che's moral incentives. In the autumn of 1965 Che told Fidel that he wanted to go away to start the liberation of Latin America from a base in Argentina or the central point of Bolivia. Fidel tried to dissuade him, then began to help him to plan the new guerrilla insurrection.

Che was not the only one of the fighters from the Sierra Maestra who wanted to fight again. As Oniria Gutiérrez, a member of Che's column, recalled, 'There were some among us who always used to say that, once we had won against Batista, we would have to go and fight in other countries.'[1] Moreover, the idea of the continuing fight against imperialism was an ideal shared by all the guerrilla leaders. As Che would write in his farewell letter to Fidel, 'Other nations are calling for the aid of my modest efforts. I can do what you are unable to do because of your responsibility as Cuban leader.'[2] In this statement Che seemed to be commiserating with Fidel because Fidel could not do what both felt ought to be done. Yet Che was middle-aged and asthmatic, softened by years of administration, when he decided to return to active combat. Except for Garibaldi and Zapata, few revolutionary leaders had left power to go out and fight again. Like Garibaldi and Zapata, Che went out to struggle and fail. And like the other two leaders, his doomed action turned him into a folk hero of his time.

However, there was more good sense than romanticism or boredom in Che's decision. He had an immense prestige; his presence in the field was worth a regiment. The world revolutionary movement was a daily sight in Cuba, which was crawling with schools for guerrilla training, political exiles, congresses for insurrection. The whole country was being run on something like a war footing by men in military kit; the national mood was a state of siege. Che was merely the most important man among many who felt impelled to return to the field of combat.

Some 1,000 Cubans were killed in the ten years after their victory against Batista while engaged in revolutions abroad. Seventeen Cubans would leave for Bolivia with Che, some of them veterans from the Sierra Maestra days. Of these, four were *comandantes*, the highest rank in the Cuban army; four were also members of the Central Committee of the Cuban Communist Party, the most responsible political positions in the island; two were over forty years old; one was a Vice Minister, one Director of Mines. In a nation which sent out its chief executives to fight from the jungles, Che's example was not unique. The Bolivian rebellion was a risk worth taking for a small island that felt itself isolated in its hemisphere. Cuba needed one, two, or three other Cubas nearby.

Che also had a personal reason for going. He was an Argentine, however much he could protest that he felt at home anywhere, and Argentina was still capitalist and unreformed. With Che's blessing, a fellow countryman called Jorge Masetti had left in 1963 with thirty men – some of them Cubans – to initiate the liberation of Argentina from the jungles in the north. They had failed to link up with the local Socialist and Communist Parties or to come to an understanding with Perón's supporters. After ten months of futile floundering and growing hysteria, Masetti's force had been decimated and dispersed by the Argentine army. This debacle had affected Che, who had hoped that Masetti would prepare the way for his later coming. In fact, Masetti had called himself by the *nom de guerre* of *Comandante Segundo*, the second-in-command. Che felt that he had to avenge Masetti's failure, although he was not responsible for it, any more than Fidel was to be responsible for Che's own failure in Bolivia. Yet decisive support could not be given to an isolated guerrilla force in its early stages. The force was completely on its own and its survival was its own business.

The time had also come for Che to leave Cuba. He had to take responsibility for the failure of the early Cuban economic policy. The Russians and other East Europeans underwriting the Cuban economy were finding this support a heavy drain on their own economies and were pressurizing Fidel to put his house in order. The Russians wanted the Cubans to go back to supplying sugar in exchange for Russian goods and credit, and to encourage material incentives in industry. Che could never accept such policies, so he chose to go on his travels again.

Everything conspired to send Che to war a second time. In 1963, he had told *El Moujahid*, an organ of the Algerian government, that the Latin American revolution was his favourite theme. Efficient and direct himself, he could not stand the inefficiency and complexity of Cuban bureaucracy any longer. As he wrote in 1964 about a government commission, 'Since it is a commission, and since it is a government commission, it will surely dawdle and accomplish nothing'.[3] He was certainly nostalgic for the simpler actions and plain results of guerrilla fighting. In his farewell letter to Fidel, he wrote of leaving Cuba 'with mixed feelings of joy and sorrow', and referred to his disillusionment with administration in the ambiguous phrase, 'I leave behind the purest of my hopes as a builder'. Above all Che felt himself a crusader of commitment, and that was the fundamental motive for his going. As he would declare finally to Fidel, he had to fulfil 'the most sacred of duties: to fight against imperialism wherever it may be'.[4] And this he did.

When Fidel came to speak a eulogy on Che after his death, he stated: 'In the future, high above any other, will be Che's example. National flags, prejudices, chauvinism and egoism had disappeared from his mind and heart.'[5] This had not been true, however, between 1959 and 1964, when Che had been the faithful servant of the Cuban state, serving as an ambassador and defending Cuban policy wherever he went. Che had faithfully followed the Cuban line in international diplomacy, as it passed from psychological warfare with the United States to the encouragement of guerrilla movements in Latin America to an alliance with the Eastern bloc Communist countries. In these six years the expatriate and internationalist Che seemed to have submerged himself in his honorary Cuban nationality.

By 1964, however, Che had rediscovered his old commitment to the poor nations of the world, if he had ever lost it. He began to consider that the real contradiction was not between capitalism and Communism, but between developed and underdeveloped countries. Disappointment with the terms exacted by Russia and Eastern Europe for their aid to Cuba turned Che towards the concept of a Third World, made up of the poor nations from three continents, Africa, Asia and Latin America. Two other worlds opposed this Third World, a Western world and an Eastern world. Both of these two worlds consisted of powerful blocs of developed countries with high standards of living, even if they claimed to be political foes. Underdevelopment and hunger drew a different frontier, dividing the haves from the have-nots, the manufacturers of goods from the suppliers of raw materials, the white-skinned peoples from the dark-skinned, the colonial powers from their old possessions. The line did not clearly divide one country from another in every case, but each drawing of the line defined more clearly a Third World set apart from the Western and Eastern powers.

Che's concept of a Third World captured the popular imagination as completely as the concepts of the Yellow Peril or Manifest Destiny did in their time. This idea would lead to ways of thought, even to diplomatic groupings. And that was Che's intention, as he set it out in a speech to the United Nations Conference on Trade and Development in March 1964. The poor nations must not squabble for loans from the rich nations. They must show solidarity.

> If the groups of underdeveloped countries, lured by the siren song of the vested interests of the developed powers which exploit their backwardness, contend futilely among themselves for the crumbs from the table of the world's

mighty and break the ranks of numerically superior forces
. . . the world will remain as it is.[6]

The poor nations had to learn not to undercut one
another in supplying raw materials, nor to take
bribes for joining either the Eastern or the Western
bloc. Che was preaching almost the virtues of a
labour union to the poor nations. In union lay
strength and bargaining power; a scab nation was a
villain. And his words had particular meaning for
those peoples who saw themselves as Frantz Fanon's
'wretched of the earth' from the Third World, rather
than as the 'wretched' hymned in the *Internationale*,
the poor workers of the industrial nations.

In a speech to the General Assembly of the
United Nations in December 1964 Che took a more
aggressive stance. He hinted that he was losing faith
in peaceful solutions involving pacts, trade
agreements, negotiations and foreign aid. These
would not resolve the conflict between the poor
and the rich. He declared, 'As Marxists we have
maintained that peaceful coexistence among nations
does not include coexistence between the
exploiters and the exploited, the oppressor and the
oppressed.'[7] This sentence was an explicit attack on
the new Russian attempt to achieve 'peaceful
coexistence' with the United States, after Kennedy

had made Krushchev back down on 28 October 1962 and withdraw his missiles from Cuba. That debacle had been Che's great humiliation.

Che developed his new theme even more strongly at the Afro-Asian Solidarity Conference at Algiers in February 1965. He now attacked Russian policy frontally, embarrassing the Cuban government and infuriating the Russians, who felt that they had already done too much for Cuba without having to be insulted as well. Yet they, too, had to learn that there was no gratitude in foreign aid. 'The Socialist countries', Che declared, 'have the moral duty to liquidate their tacit complicity with the exploiting nations of the West.' To Che there was no valid definition of socialism other than the abolition of men's exploitation of men. No country could build socialism without helping all countries to build socialism and to attack imperialism. 'There are no frontiers in this struggle to the death. We cannot remain indifferent in the face of what occurs in any part of the world. A victory for any one country against imperialism is our victory, just as a defeat for any one country is a defeat for all.'[8]

Che always tried to practise what he preached. His triumph and tragedy was to commit himself out of his own mouth. This was his last call to action before taking the field himself. He returned to Cuba, before leaving again to fight in the Congo against the white mercenaries who had provoked his anger. Before he left Havana, he sent his farewell message to Fidel, stating that he would try to stay true to his beliefs, whatever the final consequences. He also wrote that he had always identified with the world outcome of the Cuban Revolution. He took with him to the Congo several of his comrades from the Sierra Maestra, some of whom were to go on with him to Bolivia.

After the killing of Patrice Lumumba on 17 January 1961, there had been sporadic rebellions in the Congo to seize power for and from the European mining interests which controlled the new governments. These finally resulted in the dictatorship of Sese Seko Mobutu. Secession failed in Katanga, and the revolution was continued by groups in the east operating from Rwanda–Burundi under a Committee of National Liberation – one of its members, Laurent Kabila, would use that same base for a successful conquest of the Congo thirty years on. In the west Pierre Mulele was fighting: he had been Lumumba's Minister of Education and would end in pieces, fed to the crocodiles of the River Congo. By the time Che arrived in this heart of darkness, Belgian and South African units had already defeated and contained both the eastern and western independence movements.

Che could hardly see the hopelessness of his chosen guerrilla role in Africa, although Gamal Abdel Nasser in Egypt had told him that his efforts to command African troops would make him look like Tarzan. With 130 of the more black Cuban troops and pilots he could find, Che disappeared for a year from Havana in the March of 1965 on his secret expedition to Central Africa. Working with Kabila's forces in Rwanda and the Congo, Che taught them some military skills and medicine, only to find that they believed in *dawa*, a magic potion blessed by witchdoctors that deflected bullets. Ill from tropical fever and dysentery, in June Che heard of his mother's death of cancer in Buenos Aires without being able to join her. He now knew he could contribute little to the African revolution, noting in his journal, 'The main defect in the Congolese is that they don't know how to shoot'.[9] His own Cuban troops also fell ill and were badly disciplined. Reports were reaching Fidel that Che felt like a condemned gladiator, and then Fidel released Che's farewell letter to explain that his comrade had relinquished all his ministerial posts and even his Cuban citizenship. He had given up everything on a hopeless mission, and Fidel appeared to have publicized his chosen end.

Under assaults from the South African mercenaries, Che's Congolese troops ran away, and the morale of his Cuban special forces was shattered. On 21 November 1965 Che was forced to retreat, too, on an evacuation fleet of small boats across Lake Tanganyika. He emerged, as he wrote, believing more than ever in guerrilla warfare; 'but we failed'.

At the time that Che was preparing to leave the Congo, a Bolivian guerrilla fighter named Coco Peredo was buying a farm on the Nancahuazú river in southern Bolivia to serve as a base for a rising against the government of General Barrientos. The head of the Bolivian Communist Party, Mario Monje, had discussed with Fidel Castro plans to make this area the focus for a continental revolution in Latin America, although it had been a military zone for thirty years. When Che secretly returned to Cuba in the autumn of 1966 after a long and futile exile in the Cuban embassy in Dar-es-Salaam, where his wife Aleida joined him, and also in Prague, various members of the guerrilla force were filtering into the country while arms and supplies were being stockpiled in Santa Cruz and La Paz. Che himself left for Bolivia at the end of October to begin a war that he hoped would liberate Argentina and the whole of his continent from the rule of imperialism. He wanted to be the new Bolívar and be even more successful than the Great Liberator had been. Not only would he expel the power of imperialism, but he would also unite Latin America in a socialist bloc.

While he was still preparing his last rebellion in Bolivia in March 1967, Che sent back to Cuba a message, which was read out to the Tricontinental Solidarity Organization. In it Che delivered his credo before his death, his summary of a philosophy gained by spending so long in fighting for the poor peoples of the earth. He began by asking if there really had been twenty-one years of relative peace after the end of the Second World War. The struggle in Vietnam, for instance, had been continuing for nearly thirty years, while the people there had fought three imperialist powers in turn – Japan, France and the United States. The Vietnamese were still suffering the bombing and escalation of war by the Americans, who were guilty of aggression. Yet this guilt also applied to those 'who, when the time came for definition, hesitated to make Vietnam an inviolable part of the socialist world; running, of course, the risks of war on a global scale – but also forcing a decision upon imperialism'. Without naming Russia or China directly, Che continued to accuse the two Communist superpowers of quarrelling with each other and of splitting the anti-

imperialist forces of the world. Only the heroism of
the Vietnamese in fighting for themselves had dropped
the 'Great Society' of the United States into a cesspool
and had convinced the North Americans that murder
was no longer a good business for monopolies.

What could the Third World countries do, then,
if the threat of an atomic world war caused a
stalemate between the advanced Communist and
capitalist countries and permitted the genocide in
Vietnam? Che's answer was that the threat should be
ignored. 'Since imperialists blackmail humanity by
threatening it with war, the wise reaction is not to
fear war.' Latin America, Africa and Asia must
liberate themselves at any price. In Asia and Africa a
continental revolution was delayed, but in Latin
America it had already begun from its focal points
in the guerrilla groups operating in Guatemala,
Colombia, Venezuela, Peru and Bolivia. Yet if these
focal points were to become real battle-grounds,
then the United States would be forced to intervene
with modern weapons and to commit its regular
troops. This was the way to help the Vietnamese
struggle and to humble the United States.

> It is the road of Vietnam; it is the road that should be
> followed by the people; it is the road that will be followed
> in Our America. The Cuban Revolution will today have

the job of . . . creating a Second or the Third Vietnam of the world.[10]

As imperialism was a world system it could only be defeated by a global confrontation, an international attack on the chief capitalist power, the United States. Vietnam had proved that the armed forces of the United States were vulnerable to guerrillas fighting for their own country. A fierce ideology could beat the most advanced technology. Morale was the weak point of the North Americans, who were otherwise formidable fighters. Battles would be bloody against them and useless sacrifices might be unavoidable, but only fighting could defeat the economic imperialism of the United States.

These battles shall not be mere street fights with stones against tear-gas bombs, or pacific general strikes; neither shall the battle be that of a furious people destroying in two or three days the repressive scaffolds of the ruling oligarchies; the struggle shall be long and harsh, and its front shall be in the guerrillas' hide-out, in the cities, in the homes of the fighters . . . in the massacred rural population, in the villages and cities destroyed by the bombardments of the enemy.

They are pushing us into this struggle; there is no alternative; we must prepare it and we must decide to undertake it.[11]

The beginnings of the struggle were bound to be hard, but the only way to help Vietnam was to wage total war on the North Americans. No Yankee soldier should feel safe in his quarters, in the cinema, on the town. He had to be made to feel like a cornered beast and, as he behaved more and more like a beast, so his decadence would provoke his own downfall. All must fight together in a true proletarian internationalism. To die under the flag of Vietnam or Venezuela or Guinea or Bolivia would be 'equally glorious and desirable for an American, an Asian, an African or even a European'. By fighting and dying to liberate another's country, each man was helping to liberate his own. The time for controversy between Third World groups was over. All had to combine to fight against the common imperialist enemy, the United States, which was itself beginning to break up internally in a class and race war.

> Wherever death may surprise us, let it be welcome, provided that this, our battle-cry, may have reached some receptive ear, and another hand may be extended to wield our weapons, and other men be ready to intone the funeral dirge with the staccato chant of the machine-gun and new battle-cries of war and victory.[12]

So in October 1966 Che went to fight and die in Bolivia.

SEVEN

DEATH AND INFLUENCES

The *Bolivian Diary* of Che Guevara was his most immediate and human statement. Scribbled each day for eleven months during an impossible struggle for survival against jungle and mountain and isolation and a trained enemy, the diary showed no dwindling towards defeat. It revealed the bare, forked, unaccommodated Che. The rhetoric was gone, the nobility, the jargon, the dialectic. There remained only the record of a great man, trying to keep his men moving and fighting as he advanced on his own death. Like another masterpiece, *Robinson Crusoe*, the record was full of the catalogues of survival, the details of weapons and food and distances and supplies. The hardship and the endurance, the courage and the comradeship went unsaid. They lived in the spaces between the lines.

March 15, 1967

Only we, the centre party, crossed the river, with the help of el Rubio and the Doctor. We wanted to get to the mouth of the Nancahuazú River, but three of the men cannot swim and we are heavily laden. The current carried us along nearly a kilometre, and the raft could not be used as we intended. Eleven of us stayed on this side and tomorrow the Doctor and el Rubio will cross again. We shot four hawks for our meal; they were not as bad as might be imagined. Everything had got soaked and the weather continues to be very wet. The men's morale is low: Miguel has swollen feet and some of the others suffer from the same condition. Height – 580 metres.[1]

So the account of a random and average day for the guerrillas, with only an occasional death or ambush to vary the hard monotony. A recorded emotion was as rare as a victory against the enemy regiments surrounding the thirty guerrillas. When Tuma or other comrades from the old Sierra Maestra days were killed, Che set down the loss with a brevity that is unbearably moving.

With Tuma I lost an inseparable comrade in all the preceding years; he was loyal to the last, and I shall feel his absence from now onward, almost as if I had lost a son. When he fell, he asked them to give me his watch . . . I will wear it throughout the war. We put the body on an animal and took it away to bury far from there.

Heroic tragedy demands a sense of inevitable fate. Throughout the *Bolivian Diary* the presence of death broods. Che did not go to fight in Bolivia to get himself killed; but he knew that the odds were against his survival. After all, the beginning of the Cuban campaign had taught him that the whole group could easily be wiped out in the opening stages, as had nearly happened at Alegría de Pío. Luck had to aid the guerrilla group as well as skill at keeping alive. And luck ran out for Che in Bolivia.

Because Che was killed and because the Bolivian insurrection failed, many commentators were wise after the event. There were factors which made a success in Bolivia more unlikely than in Cuba. First, Che and the other guerrilla leaders were Cubans, while revolution in Latin America had always had a strong nationalistic streak. There was friction within the guerrilla group itself between the Cubans and their Bolivian comrades, while the Bolivian Indians not only distrusted the Cubans as foreigners, but also as another lot of lying white men. Secondly, Bolivia had had a land reform during its previous left-wing régime: the Bolivian Indians might be miserably poor, but they did own their own barren soil for the first time in 300 years, and an acre in the hand was worth any utopia in the bush. Che's total failure to recruit one single peasant to the guerrilla cause during his eleven months of preparation and fighting was the basic cause of his defeat. As he had stated in his own book, *Guerrilla Warfare*, the fundamental reason for the success in Cuba had been the aid of the peasants in the Sierra Maestra. 'To try and carry out this kind of war without the support of the population is the prelude to inevitable disaster.'[3]

Other factors doomed the guerrillas' campaign. Isolation was the worst blow. The middle-class sympathizers in the large cities were soon betrayed by three of the weaker guerrillas, who defected. Parallel risings in Peru and other Latin American countries fizzled out, through a failure of nerve and communications. Che could not now bring himself to be ruthless enough to kill potential traitors both inside and outside of the guerrilla force. As a result, his base camp fell into enemy hands with the loss of vital asthma medicines and supplies and papers. Also lost was the cover of the local intermediary and Russian or East German agent, Tania, who was attached to Che, even though she probably informed on him to her paymasters. Then Che split his own small force into two parts, which were hunted down and destroyed separately. A certain resignation and lack of aggression in Che as a commander also began to show itself, as he grew physically sick and weak. Once he even became hysterical enough to stab a faithful mare. His heroism lay in his unceasing struggle against the sight of his own and his group's decomposition. As long as he could stand, he would fight on.

Internal politics in Bolivia contributed to Che's defeat. General Barrientos was, after all, a Bolivian. And although Che could rightly accuse him of accepting North American arms and advisers, Barrientos could justifiably accuse the guerrillas of being wholly led and supplied by Cuban Communists. Fidel had refused to take non-Cubans on the *Granma* except for Che, because his rebellion might be seen as a foreign invasion. Che was not so wise. Moreover, Che's greatest failure lay in his lack of suppleness as a politician. He had to compromise with one man, Mario Monje, to end his isolation and to stop his group being strangled by vastly superior forces. Monje was head of the Bolivian Communist Party and Che had to have his help in fomenting unrest in the mines and in La Paz. Fidel in Cuba had been shifty about the pledges he gave to urban politicians to get their support; Che coolly dismissed Fidel's later reneging on his promises with the words:

> We were not satisfied with this compromise, but it was
> necessary; at that time it was progressive. It could not last
> beyond the time when it became a brake on revolutionary
> development, but we were willing to go along with it.

Yet Che would not compromise. When Monje demanded that the Bolivian Communist Party lead the insurrection as the price of its support, Che stated that he had to be the chief. In fact, he would have been the leader in practice, fighting in isolation in the jungles and mountains, but he had to be the theoretical commander as well. That was the Cuban creed; the actual guerrillas should lead. Monje had, anyway, betrayed his promises to Fidel that the Bolivian Communist Party would back Che on any terms. Che was the field commander; he had to lead, by his own theory. Che would rather die than deny himself.

Despite these difficulties and errors, however, the Bolivian insurrection could have overthrown the Barrientos government. The original theory of the Cuban Revolution, that the revolution made itself and that conditions were never good enough for rational men to start a revolution, nearly received a second startling confirmation. After the surprising rebel attack on Sumaipata in July 1967, when a few guerrillas captured a whole town and its garrison, the Barrientos government tottered. The legend of the guerrillas led by Che caused both Argentina and Peru to close their frontiers and to mobilize their troops. Apparently, Bolivia was becoming the focus for a continental revolution, particularly as there had been a spontaneous rising in June in the Bolivian mines, which the army had suppressed with great brutality. Had Che been more aggressive at this moment and attacked with his twenty-two remaining men the defenceless Bolivian oilfields and communications, the growing legend of the invincible guerrillas would have brought in recruits and might well have caused the downfall of Barrientos, who had many enemies waiting to capitalize on popular discontent. Yet Che was too cautious, the quality of the Bolivian army's strategy began to improve and the handful of guerrillas began to fall into the ambushes they had previously been so clever in setting. During the last three months of his campaign, Che was on the run and losing. His rearguard was wiped out trying to ford the Rio Grande, and Tania was killed.

Even the later disaster at the Yuro Ravine in October 1967, when the wounded Che was himself captured and his group dispersed, was hardly worse than the debacle at Alegría de Pío. Ten men survived the disaster, although five of these were later rounded up by the Bolivian army. Of the others, three of the Cubans reached safety in Chile, and the leading Bolivian guerrilla, Inti Peredo, turned back into Bolivia with invincible optimism to continue the struggle, sending out a dispatch which stated:

> Guerrilla warfare in Bolivia is not dead! It has just begun . . . We are convinced that the dream of Bolívar and Che – that of uniting Latin America both politically and geographically – will be attained through armed struggle, which is the only dignified, honest, glorious and irreversible method which will motivate the people.

The care that the Bolivian army authorities took to assassinate the wounded Che showed the fear that the military governments of Latin America felt about Che's dream of uniting the continent through armed struggle. They knew that his cause would not die with his body. They might inter his corpse, but they could not bury his ideal. Che was executed on 9 October 1967 in a schoolhouse by six shots to the body and his remains were flown by helicopter to Vallegrande, where they were washed, photographed and displayed to prove that the legendary guerrilla commander was really dead. On the next day Che's hands were amputated and preserved, to be taken later to Cuba by a Bolivian army defector in return for asylum. In July 1997 his bones, along with those of other assassinated comrades, were dug up alongside the airstrip at Vallegrande. They were returned to Fidel Castro in Cuba, where the Argentine *comandante* received the state burial of a glorious hero.

Yet Fidel had not tried to rescue Che, once his isolation and the loss of his rearguard meant that the mission was doomed. He had been brought back from his failure in the Congo and his exile in Tanzania in the Cuban Embassy. On this occasion, however, he was left to wither in the jungle until his execution. A rescue expedition from Havana would have been difficult or impossible; but it was never mounted. The reason was Russian fury at the Bolivian adventure and at Cuban efforts to spread the revolution to Latin America, while the Soviets were seeking better relations with the United States and feuding against China, which Che supported. The Kremlin, indeed, finally persuaded the Bolivian Communist leader, Mario Monje, to withhold all support from the Cuban *comandante*. And that was Che's last hope gone.

In death Che had more influence than when alive. Dead men may tell no tales, but they can make a legend. Che was not only one of the more courageous men of his age; he was also one of the more intelligent, more original, more ascetic, more radical, more human and more beautiful men of that time. His face launched a thousand turmoils, his words a hundred revolts. He provided the Marxists with a kind of saint, who dedicated his life and death to the poorest of men without help from God. His martyrdom was the condition for his inspiration of the young.

Che's death was the prelude to the full fury of the Red Guard movement in Mao's China and the Tet offensive of the Vietcong in South Vietnam. With Che as their personal symbol and the Red Guards as their general model, many of the world's students revolted in the turbulent summer of 1968. The events of that year were curiously similar to those of 1848, when a wave of insurrection swept through the capital cities of Europe and ended in victory for the powers that were. The chief difference between the student revolts of 1968 and the middle-class revolts of 1848 lay in the new inspiration.

Both Che and the Red Guards were inspired by the concept of a rural revolt that would sweep out of the countryside to purge the corruption of the cities. The middle-class students who fought in the streets of Paris during the May Revolution, or in Chicago during the Democratic Convention, or in Berlin or London or Buenos Aires or Tokyo or Mexico City or twenty other cities during the year after Che's death, came from an urban or suburban setting. They did not want to know of their misconception of Che's and Mao's thought. Yet Mao would remind them, when he sent 20 million of the Red Guards back to labour in the countryside. And Che's end, too, had been the result of a middle-class doctor and guerrilla failing to win over the poor farmers and miners of Bolivia.

The governments of the world won in 1968. In Communist and capitalist countries, in developed and in underdeveloped countries, the protest of the young was defeated by the power of the old. In Latin America nearly all the guerrilla risings were suppressed. Harsher measures were taken in Kenya as well as in Czechoslovakia, in Mexico as well as in France, in China as well as in the United States. This was a global reaction against an international revolt partially inspired by Che's death. But just as Bolívar failed five times before succeeding in Latin America, and Che himself failed three times in Guatemala and the Congo and Bolivia for his one success in Cuba, so the crushing of the revolts of 1968 did not mean the end of them. For Che's most explosive idea was that the revolution was permanent and that the revolution created itself.

In every cult there is an element of the untrue and the irrational. In the case of Che, that element is his identification with Christ: many student posters of him put a halo round his head. Because he fought for the poor and because he chose to be sacrificed in his prime, he gave a mystical impression that he died for all humanity. Clearly, he killed and executed other men. Clearly, he hated his enemies. Clearly, his beliefs stemmed from political doctrines loathsome to many. Clearly, he advocated and used tactics that were sometimes dubious or inhuman. Clearly, he was a man who lived in his muck and sweat, like a beast in the jungle. Yet clearly, he transcended all these facts.

Che appeared as much larger than a human being, as somebody approaching a saviour. When all was said and done, when his words and acts had been coldly seen and sometimes condemned, the conviction remained that Che was always driven by his love for humanity and for the ultimate good of mankind. The ideals expressed in his writings, his whole life and his passion and his death transcended ideology. The photograph of his corpse became an icon in many country homes across Catholic Latin America.

Sartre was correct when he called Che 'the most complete man of his age'. There was a Renaissance quality about Che; he had more careers in his thirty-nine years than a whole squad of men might have in their lives, and he had more lives than any litter of cats. He tried to be professional in everything he did, as a doctor, a diarist, a political and military theorist, a guerrilla fighter, an economist, a tactician, a banker, a planner, an industrialist, an ambassador, or a propagandist.

Yet Che was complete in more than his work. He was all of a piece. He seems to have had hardly any contradictions or inner conflicts. He was amazingly consistent in all he said and thought and did in his maturity. The professional administrator who discussed the economy of Latin America was no different from the guerrilla hero in Bolivia, who had decided that combat was the only way of solving his continent's social and economic problems. The difference between Che and other men was that Che did not let other men put his ideas into practice. He practised them himself.

There was no duality between Che's actions and his words. The writer performed what he preached, and put other intellectuals to shame. The man of action set down his experiences and analysed them to draw practical and moral conclusions from them. The dreamer applied his skills in trying to make his dreams concrete. Che was an absolutist. He wanted to pursue everything to its just conclusion. His consistency was almost maddening in its effortlessness. There was no trace of hypocrisy in him. When he said that working for one's fellow men was the greatest joy a man could have, that was true for him. He thought it was fit for a revolutionary to go and die under the flag of a nation not yet born, and he did so, not making a great display of courage, but being brave and cheerful as if he were doing the most natural thing in the world. He said that no one was irreplaceable and felt that this applied to him as much as to anyone else. So he exposed himself and died. He was a complete man.

The recent revival of Che's image as an advertising tool for promoting holidays in Havana was only a sad proof of how Marshall McLuhan's slogan of the 1960s – 'The medium is the message' – became thirty years later 'The medium is the message and the market'. The collapse of Russian Communism and the loss of its Eastern European empire led to withdrawal of its support from Cuba, forcing Fidel's island into a truce with capitalism. Fidel finally had to forego Che's ideals to supply his people. The face on the proliferating Guevara T-shirts did not display what his living and dying showed. The Revolution was turned into radical chic. The resurrection of Che's beard and beret killed the content of his days. Marxism finally expired in merchandise.

History will probably treat Guevara as the Garibaldi of his age, the most admired and beloved revolutionary of his time. The impact of his ideas on socialism and guerrilla warfare may be temporary, but his influence, particularly in Latin America, must be lasting. For there has been no man with so great an ideal of unity for that divided and unlucky continent since Bolívar. When the general in the film of *Viva Zapata* looks down at the riddled corpse of the dead guerrilla leader, he says, 'Sometimes a dead man can be a terrible enemy'. For the rich nations of the earth, and for the corrupt governments that rule many of the poor nations, the dead Che Guevara remains a terrible and a beautiful enemy.

NOTES

CHAPTER ONE

1. Speech of Che Guevara, Havana, 1967, quoted in Andrew Sinclair, *Guevara* (London, Collins, 1970), p. 7. All translations are from the original Spanish.

2. Ibid., p. 7 See also Ricardo Rojo, *My Friend Che* (New York, Dial Press, 1968), *passim*.

3. Ibid. The classmate was Alberto Granado, who wrote of Guevara in *Con el Che por Sudamerica* (Havana, Editorial Letras Cubanas, 1980).

4. Ibid., p. 8. The teacher was Elba Rossi de Oviedo Zelaya.

5. Ibid. This remark was made by Che Guevara to Alberto Granado in December 1943.

6. Ibid. Che's aunt Beatriz also talked to Jon Lee Anderson of Che's years at university, *Che Guevara: A Revolutionary Life* (London, Bantam Press, 1997).

7. 19 August 1960. Translated from *Obra Revolucionaria*, Año 1960, No. 24, Havana.

8. Mario Monje to Jorge Castañeda on 1 November 1995, in Moscow, reproduced in Jorge Castañeda, *Compañero: The Life and Death of Che Guevara* (London, Bloomsbury, 1997), p. 58.

9. Sinclair, *Guevara*, p. 11.

10. Ibid., pp. 11–12.

11. Che Guevara to Tito Infante, 8 October 1954.

12. Sinclair, *Guevara*, p. 15. See also Régis Debray, *La Guerrilla de Che* (Paris, Maspéro, 1974).

13. Hilda Gadea, *Ernesto: A Memoir of Che Guevara* (London, W.H. Allen, 1973), p. 51.

14. Sinclair, *Guevara*, pp. 16–17. This was part of Castro's eulogy of Guevara, delivered on 18 October 1967.

CHAPTER TWO

1. Sinclair, *Guevara*, p. 19.

2. Ibid.

3. Ibid., p. 20.

4.   Ibid., p. 20–1. See also Guevara's speech on 8 October 1960, 'We Are Practical Revolutionaries,' in *Venceremos!: The Speeches and Writings of Ernesto Che Guevara* (edited, annotated, and with an introduction by John Gerassi, London, Weidenfeld & Nicolson, 1968), pp. 120–6.

5.   Ibid., p. 21. The campaign in the Sierra Maestra is fully discussed by Guevara in his *Guerrilla Warfare* (Lincoln and London, University of Nebraska Press, 1985).

6.   Ibid., p. 22.

7.   Ibid., p. 25.

8.   Ibid. See also Che Guevara, *Episodes of the Cuban Revolutionary War* (New York, Pathfinder, 1996), originally pubished as *Pasajes de la Guerra Revolucionaria* (Havana, 1963).

9.   Ibid., p. 27.

CHAPTER THREE

1.   From *Verde Olivo*, 8 October 1960. Guevara and Mao Zedong's theories were later published with a foreword by Captain B.H. Liddell Hart as *Guerrilla Warfare* (London, Cassell, 1962).

CHAPTER FOUR

1.   Sinclair, *Guevara*, p. 46.

2.   Ibid., pp. 52–3.

3.   Ibid., p. 53. See also Che Guevara's speech 'On Growth and Imperialism' at the 'Alliance for Progress' meeting, 8 August 1961, *Venceremos!*, pp. 153–81. In that book, there are also reproduced important speeches by Guevara 'On Economic Planning in Cuba', pp. 139–52, and 'Our Industrial Tasks', pp. 190–203.

CHAPTER FIVE

1.   Guevara's farewell letter to Castro, summer 1965, read by Castro during a speech on 3 October 1965.

2.   Sinclair, *Guevara*, p. 58. See also Guevara's speeches on the Cuban economy in *Venceremos!*

3.   Ibid., p. 61.

4.   Ibid., pp. 61–2.

5.   Ibid., p. 63.

6.   Che Guevara, 'Man and Socialism in Cuba', a letter from Africa

to Carlos Quijano, editor-publisher of the Uruguayan weekly, *Marcha*, written early in 1965, and quoted by Sinclair, *Guevara*, pp. 64–9.

CHAPTER SIX

1. Sinclair, *Guevara*, p. 72.
2. See note 1, Chapter 5.
3. Sinclair, *Guevara*, p. 74.
4. See note 1, Chapter 5.
5. See note 14, Chapter 1.
6. Guevara, 'On Development'. A speech delivered at the plenary session of the United Nations Conference on Trade and Development on 25 March 1964. The full text is reproduced in *Venceremos!*, pp. 317–35. The quotation is from Sinclair, *Guevara*, p. 76.
7. Guevara, 'Colonialism is Doomed'. A speech delivered before the General Assembly of the United Nations on 11 December 1964. The full text is reproduced in *Venceremos!*, pp. 364–77. The quotation is from Sinclair, *Guevara*, p. 76.
8. Guevara, 'On Our Common Aspiration – The Death of Imperialism and the Birth of a Moral World'. A speech delivered in Algiers at the Afro-Asian Solidarity Conference on 26 February 1965. The full text is reproduced in *Venceremos!*, pp. 378–86. The quotation is from Sinclair, *Guevara*, pp. 77–8.
9. Guevara's journal, May summary, 1965, quoted in Castañeda, *Compañero*, p. 308.
10. Guevara, 'Create two, three . . . many Vietnams'. A message to the Tricontinental Solidarity Organisation, published in Havana, 16 April 1967. The full text is reproduced in *Venceremos!*, pp. 413–24. The quotations are from Sinclair, *Guevara*, pp. 80–2.
11. Ibid.
12. Ibid.

CHAPTER SEVEN

1. Guevara, *Bolivian Diary* (London, Lorrimer, 1968), p. 61.
2. Ibid., p. 108–9.
3. Sinclair, *Guevara*, p. 85.
4. Ibid., p. 86.
5. Inti Peredo, July 1968, Bolivia.

BIBLIOGRAPHY

Alexandre, Marianne, ed., *Viva Che!* London, Lorrimer, Third World Series, 1968. Without her original help, this biography could not have been written.

Alvarez Batista, Gerónimo, *Che: Una Neuva Batalla*. Havana, Pablo de la Torriente, 1994.

Anderson, Jon Lee, *Che Guevara: A Revolutionary Life*. London, Bantam Press, 1997.

Ariet, María del Carmen, *Che: Pensamiento Politico*. Havana: Editora Política, 1993.

Castañeda, Jorge G., *Compañero: The Life and Death of Che Guevara*. London, Bloomsbury, 1997.

Castro, Fidel, *Che: A Memoir by Fidel Castro*. Melbourne, Australia, Ocean Press, 1994.

Castro, Fidel and Guevara Che, *To Speak the Truth*. New York, Pathfinder, 1992.

Centro de Estudios Sobre América, *Pensar al Che*, Tomo 1 and 2. Havana, Editorial José Martí, 1989.

Debray, Régis, *La Guerrilla de Che*. Paris, Maspéro, 1974.

Franqui, Carlos, *Cuba: Le Livre des Douze*. Paris, Gallimard, 1968.

Gadea, Hilda, *Ernesto: A Memoir of Che Guevara: An Intimate Account of the Making of a Revolutionary by His First Wife, Hilda Gadea*. London, W.H. Allen, 1973.

Galvarro, Carlos Soria, *El Che en Bolivia: Documentos y Testimonios*, vols. 1–5. La Paz, Bolivia, CEDOIN Colección Historia y Documento, 1992–6.

Bibliography

González, Luis J., and Gustavo A. Sánchez Salazár, *The Great Rebel: Che Guevara in Bolivia*. New York, Grove Press, 1969.

Granado, Alberto, *Con el Che por Sudamerica*. Havana, Editorial Letras Cubanas, 1980.

Guevara, Ernesto Che, *Bolivian Diary*. Trans. Carlos P. Hansen and Andrew Sinclair. London, Jonathan Cape/Lorrimer, 1968.

——. *Episodes of the Cuban Revolutionary War*. New York, Pathfinder, 1996.

——. *Guerrilla Warfare*. Lincoln and London, University of Nebraska Press, 1985.

——. *Ideario Político y Filosófico del Che*. Havana, Editora Politica/Olivo Colección, 1991.

——. *The Motorcycle Diaries*. London, Verso, 1994.

——. *Venceremos!: The Speeches and Writings of Ernesto Che Guevara*. Ed. John Gerassi. London, Weidenfeld & Nicolson, 1968.

Guevara Lynch, Ernesto, *Aquí Va un Soldado de las Américas*. Sudamericana-Planeta, 1987.

——. *Mí Hijo el Che*. Havana, Editorial Arte, 1988.

Harris, Richard L., *Death of a Revolutionary: Che Guevara's Last Mission*. New York, Norton, 1970.

James Daniel, *Che Guevara: A Biography*. New York, Stein and Day, 1969.

Larteguy, Jean, *Los Guerrilleros*. Mexico, Editorial Diana, 1979.

Matthews, Herbert L., *The Cuban Story*. New York, George Braziller, 1961.

——. *Castro: A Political Biography.* London, Pelican Books, 1969.

Prado Salmón, General Gary, *The Defeat of Che Guevara*. Westport, Conn., Greenwood Press, 1990.

Bibliography

Peredo, Inti, *Mi Campana con el Che*. Mexico, Editorial Diogenes S.A., 1972.

Rojo, Ricardo, *My Friend Che*. New York, Dial Press, 1968.

Sinclair, Andrew, *Guevara*. London, Fontana/Collins, 1979.

Tablada, Carlos, Jack Barnes, Steve Clark, and Mary-Alice Waters, *Che Guevara: Cuba and the Road to Socialism*. New York, New International, 1991.

Villeges, Harry (Pombo), *Pombo: Un Hombre de la Guerrilla del Che*. Havana, Editora Política, 1996.

POCKET BIOGRAPHIES